# The Making of
# MANCHESTER

## MIKE FLETCHER

*Series Editor*
**Brian Elliott**

**Wharncliffe Books**

First Published in 2003 by
Wharncliffe Books
*an imprint of*
Pen and Sword Books Limited,
47 Church Street, Barnsley,
South Yorkshire. S70 2AS

Copyright © Michael Fletcher 2003

*For up-to-date information on other titles produced under the*
*Wharncliffe imprint, please telephone or write to:*

    Wharncliffe Books
    FREEPOST
    47 Church Street
    Barnsley
    South Yorkshire S70 2BR
    Telephone (24 hours): 01226 - 734555

## ISBN: 1-903425-32-8

A CIP catalogue record of this book is available from the
British Library

**Cover illustration:** *The Hall i' th'Wood, near Bolton.* Author's collection
**Contents page illustration:** *The Free Trade Hall, Peter Street, c.1840.* H E Tidmarsh

Printed in the United Kingdom by
CPI UK

# Contents

# $\mathscr{I}$NTRODUCTION

M anchester is a city that is famous throughout the world. When people think of the Industrial Revolution, cotton or canals, they will often picture Manchester. And yet that is just one aspect of the story that is *The Making of Manchester*.

Manchester, or *Mancunium*, was created by the Romans, when they built a fort there in the first century. Manchester, or *Maincestre*, was the home of the Anglo-Saxons, who created a settlement here from the decay that had been the remains of the Roman fort. Although Manchester was ransacked by the Danes during the ninth century, it would be rebuilt and prosper during the medieval period under the guidance of the barons of Manchester, though especially during the reign of Baron Robert Grelley. By the reign of the Tudors and Stuarts, Manchester was already trading in textiles. However, the English Civil War interrupted that trade, and saw the old town become the headquarters of the Parliamentarians and be spared the bloodshed and destruction of other urban centres in the region.

However, it was during the Hanoverian and Victorian period that Manchester really prospered, with the arrival of industry – in Manchester's case cotton mills – which in turn inspired the creation of canals, railways and warehouses. Manchester, or *Cottonopolis*, was the first industrial city. And yet, although there was employment for all, young and old alike, there was massive poverty and deprivation, where the working classes were forces to work excessively long hours, for little pay, live in squalid houses, and be denied any form of representation. These conditions led to radicals and reformers, who called for change, and although they would finally achieve their goal, it would be at a terrible price – culminating in the Peterloo Massacre of 1819.

The twentieth century brought with it much in the way of change for the residents of Manchester; better housing, a better standard of living, and state education were just some of the benefits, though the downside was having to endure the misery and suffering of two World Wars. And what of the twenty-first century, what will that have in store for Manchester?

Manchester's story is an interesting one and in many ways acts as a mirror to the changes witnessed by many other towns and cities throughout the north-west of England.

# 1 ℱOUNDATIONS

**A**LTHOUGH throughout pre-Roman Britain, there were many individual tribes that made up the Britons, within the north west region the predominant tribe were the Brigantes. Their name means 'hill dwellers', which suggests that they built their settlements initially at least, within the Pennine region. Later, of course, they must have spread out to the lowlands, and, although there is no real evidence to support this opinion, I feel certain that the Brigantes must have established a settlement at the joining of the rivers Irwell and Medlock. It was, after all, an ideal defensive position, and that is why the Romans built their fort there years later.

Whether we can refer to the Roman fort as 'the foundations of Manchester' is questionable, but it is from this period that most people equate the origins of Manchester.

The Romans landed on the shores of Britain in AD43. And, although they managed to secure control of the south of the country, they found that moving northwards was somewhat more difficult.

*Manchester's Cathedral stands on Hunt's Bank, the location of the earliest of Manchester's Roman forts which, according to Professor Charles Roeder, was built by Cerealis on one of his earlier expeditions into Brigantia.* Author's collection

They made several failed attempts: Suetonius Paulinus, lead the legions north in around AD61, reaching as far as Deva (Chester), before being recalled to defend the south from further acts. They would return to the north west – Brigantia – over a decade later, finally reaching Manchester around AD79, after General Agricola marched the Twentieth Legion from Chester, across the wastelands of the north west (crossing the fords at Stretford and Trafford en route), to engage the Brigantes. This area, at the meeting of the rivers of Irk, Medlock and Irwell, was of such strategic value, that the Romans stayed and built an equally impressive fort here, at Manchester. This region, once so difficult to conquer, would later become one of the prime centres of activity by the Romans, with Manchester playing its part, along with that of Warrington, Wigan, Ribchester and Lancaster, of course.

The initial fortification at Manchester was made of local timber, and built on a natural raised mound, that gave the settlement its Roman name, *Mamucium*: meaning a 'breast like hill'. The fort was quite substantial, covering around five acres and built to hold around five hundred men. Its location, at the meeting of the three rivers of Irwell, Medlock and Irk, held a strategic military importance as it protected the main route between the east and the west, across the Pennines, uniting Eboracum (York) to Deva. Sections of this Roman road can still be seen today: for instance, the causeway on the moors around Blackstone Edge formed sections of it.

Manchester's fort was also used to control the natives, and defend the vital supply route through to the fort at Ribchester from attack. Between them, the two forts ensured that munitions, troops and supplies continued to flow northwards, to outposts such as Galacuim (Overborough) and Glannventa (Ravenglass) on the coast, and, most importantly, the outpost at Luguvalium (Carlisle), on the very edge of the frontier, to maintain the northern defences.

As the fort gained greater importance, within a few years of its creation, it was enlarged, and completely rebuilt in stone. And, throughout the Roman occupation the fort would continue to grow in overall stature, with further rebuilding and enlargements occurring during the Trajan and Hadrian periods.

Although the north west region was not as open to attack as the settlements situated further north, Manchester's fort formed an important link in controlling the Brigantes; maintaining a strong and highly visible military presence meant that a rebellion was less likely and could be quelled quickly should it ever arise. Nevertheless, despite its stature, a posting here was not popular amongst the legionnaires, for in those times the north west region was largely wasteland, consisting of moors, marshland and bogs, the climate was cold and damp, and it was a most inhospitable place.

Every day life here at Manchester would be made that little bit more hospitable for the legionnaires and their families in AD84, when, on the instructions of General Agricola, a *vicus* (settlement) was created outside the fort. Although it was not particularly large, consisting of about six streets, each of them running off a central main thoroughfare, it was self-contained, with its own mill, and large enough to accommodate several families. Although this could easily be mistaken for the beginnings of Manchester, in reality it was far from it, for the vicus didn't survive the Romans eventual departure; although in some ways it did form the foundations of Manchester, in that its stone, along with that of the fort, would be plundered and used to build the early town of Manchester in the eleventh and twelfth centuries.

Despite the work carried out here at Mamucium, once the legions were recalled to Rome, in AD410, the region underwent a period of unrest, with various local tribes and groups fighting for supremacy, and the result was that the fort fell into disuse, and its stone plundered.

**Manchester's Roman Heritage**
Throughout the centuries many travellers and writers of their day have visited the remains of what might well be described as Roman Manchester, though their views are often misleading. For instance, John Leland visited Manchester during the sixteenth century and was less than impressed with the remains of the old fort, claiming that much of it had already been plundered for building work elsewhere; however, two centuries later William Stukeley, visited Manchester and was impressed with what he saw.

Although the Roman fort at Manchester should be the pinnacle of the city's historic heritage, sadly its not, for unlike Chester, Manchester's passionate embrace of the industrial revolution caused massive damage to the Roman remains. Unfortunately, the eighteenth and nineteenth century's desire for commerce would inflict severe, irrepairable damage to this historic site: the growth of the cotton mills lead to the introduction of vital transport links, such as the canals and the railways, whose construction, taking place right in the heart of Castlefields, almost obliterated the old fort site. But, if this wasn't bad enough, further damage was to follow with the building of rows of terraced houses here in the latter years of the nineteenth century.

Despite this construction – and in some cases because of it – there

*The later Roman fort was located at Castlefield in AD 79. It was an ideal defensive position shielded by the rivers Irk and Irwell. However, the arrival of transport during the eighteenth and nineteenth centuries – namely the canals and the railways – altered Castlefield so much that the remains of the Roman forts were all but destroyed. These three modern photos show the reconstructed remains of the fort, an example of what a section of the fort might have looked like, and the impact of the canals and railways.* The Author

have been many Roman artefacts discovered throughout the centuries: a bronze statuette of Jupiter was found here during the nineteenth century, and further excavations, in around and under Knott Mill Station, has revealed more of Manchester's Roman fort, and helped archaeologists to understand more of its layout. In more recent times, there have been many attempts to uncover the lost settlement that was Roman Manchester. A section of the surrounding defensive ditch was discovered in 1951, and three years later, some of the former ramparts were unearthed off Beaufort Street, by Professor Atkinson of Manchester University. As part of the area's heritage, part of the old ramparts have been skilfully reconstructed, including the North Gate and the West Wall, and now form part of the Castlefield Urban Heritage Park, which opened to visitors in 1982.

**The Dark Ages**
After the Roman's departure, a minor settlement continued here made up of Romano-Britons, changing its name to Maineceastre: meaning simply 'the place of the fort'. In AD429 the Picts and the Scots invaded, and laid waste to the area, including the settlement of Maineceastre. The local Britons, in what we can only conclude must have been sheer desperation, summoned the assistance of the noted warriors from Saxony, who were often used as mercenaries, to fight the barbarians. The Saxons defeated the Celts and thereafter took the land for themselves; tribes of Saxons, Angles and Jutes spread throughout the country, including Maineceastre, which they later renamed Manchester: meaning 'men of the fort'.

Around this period, the Britons turned to new leaders to fight, and hopefully defeat the Saxons. From this undocumented period, stem many myths and legends of many victorious warriors, such as King Arthur, who is said to have lead many an army, in many decisive battles, against the Germanic invaders. These are nothing more than that; legends, myths, old-wives stories, and have little basis in history. Included in this is a tale often told of the settlement of Maineceastre concerning the fight that Sir Lancelot is said to have had with a giant Saxon knight, by the name of Sir Tarquin, who is supposed to have lived in the ruined Roman fort or castle on the banks of the River Medlock and had supposedly slain many knights. Sir Lancelot fought and killed Sir Tarquin, so the legend says, with the assistance of Vivian, the lady of the lake. However, despite this interesting little tale, there are no records to support it, and no record of a Saxon knight ever having lived in the ruins of the Roman fort.

### Life Beyond The Dark Ages

The Anglo-Saxons divided England into seven kingdoms. Two of the largest – Mercia and Northumbria – were situated in the north. Manchester, initially at least, was contained within the borders of Northumbria, which had been created during the sixth century. Later, sometime between the seventh and ninth centuries, the borders of Mercia and Northumbria were altered: the southern border of Northumbria became the River Ribble, so south of the river became Mercia which, of course, included the castle at Manchester.

During this period, the settlement was growing in stature once more, as it is suspected that the town's first church, dedicated to St Mary, was built around this time. And, although its location is not known for certain today, it is largely thought that it stood somewhere between the modern-day streets of St Mary and Deansgate. Again, its fate is not known for certain either, though it is thought that it was probably destroyed during the Viking invasion of the ninth century. Today the only remains are the famous Angel Stone, discovered during alterations to the cathedral in 1871.

The Vikings destroyed Manchester's church, and wrecked the town, laying it and its inhabitants to waste in AD865. The Great Army of the Danes swept throughout the country, overrunning the former kingdoms of both Northumbria and Mercia and more besides. For years much of the north of England lay in the Vikings hands. And with their capital at York, they set about creating settlements within their new kingdom; there were several of these around Manchester, such as Oldham, Hulme, Cheadle Hulme and Urmston.

Resistance eventually came from the south, lead by Alfred, King of Wessex, who engaged the enemy in battle on several occasions, slowly but surely gaining victories. This fight was continued by his children, Edward the Elder and Aethelflaed, Queen of Mercia, who succeeded in forcing the invaders back across the border of the River Mersey. To protect this new boundary a series of defensive forts, or Burhs, were established along its length, at Chester, Eddisbury and Runcorn. Later, in AD923, King Edward established two new forts at Thelwall and Manchester, respectively. This attention to Manchester brought about its rejuvenation, and having a fort on its doorstep once more made it a safe place to settle. Edward's conquest of Northumbria later that same year, finished the task in forcing the Danes to flee to their capital at York; although the final victory would be more than a decade later, in the Battle of Brunanburgh, won by his illegitimate son, Athelstan, that ended the wars once and for all.

Following the end of the conflict, Northumbria's border was reestablished at the River Ribble, though Mercia's northern border was re-drawn, this time further south, at the Mersey. The area in between was given separate status, as a Royal domain, though contained within the huge diocese of Lichfield (which it remained through to 1541). Manchester became a part of this Royal domain, referred to as *Inter Ripam et Mersham*: 'the lands between the Ribble and the Mersey'.

The Danes invaded again in 1012, this time led by King Swein, who was successful, leading to the reign of the Danish kings of England: though the prize of the first Danish king of England was not to go to Swein, who was killed in battle just prior to their overall victory, but to his son Canute. King Canute ruled England with the inclusion and co-operation of the Saxon chiefs, making life for the common people basically unaltered. Later, however, the administration of the country, which had been greatly enhanced with the creation of the earldoms, once again subdivided into smaller areas known as Wapentakes (thought to originate from both Saxon and Norse terms for weapon count, an early form of voting) later becoming more commonly referred to as Hundreds, as each area contained one hundred manors. The land between the Ribble and the Mersey was divided into six such hundreds: West Derby, Blackburn, Leyland, Newton, Warrington and Salford: Manchester was contained within the latter, it was not able to form such a hundred itself, as it was still in a ruined state from the fighting with the Danes – Salford, on the other hand, holding less importance, had been less affected. The land between the Ribble and the Mersey was still under the direct control of the ruling monarch, and would remain so until the arrival of the Normans to our shores in 1066.

### Norman England
The arrival of the Normans brought with it great changes to the way the country was administered. The former royal domain, the lands between the Ribble and the Mersey, was awarded to William's cousin, Roger de Poitou, the youngest son of Roger of Montgomery, Earl of Shrewsbury. Roger was to prove a good administrator, establishing forts and castles throughout his territory, and appointing barons to control each of the sectors. At Manchester, for instance, a new castle was built, and further streets added to the medieval town.

The start of medieval Manchester saw the town being rebuilt in the area surrounding the old Roman vicus. This was referred to as Alport, meaning old town, with the thoroughfare we know as Deansgate today being added later and called Alport Lane. The centre of the medieval town remained here through to the thirteenth century, when

Robert Grelley, the fifth baron, shifted the presence of the town around the parish church at the opposite end of Alport, creating new streets (such St Mary's Gate and Market Street) and offering 150 burgesses, all with street frontages, to attract new inhabitants. It is from this later medieval town that modern Manchester originates, with thoroughfares such as Long Millgate and Hanging Ditch.

### Barons of Manchester

Although De Poitou was a sound administrator, his loyalty to the king was questionable, and after rebelling against William he was exiled. In his absence, the Earl of Chester was appointed by the monarch to control the lands previously held by De Poitou; he in turn appointed Nigel (whose surname is uncertain, though some historians suspect it might have been Percival) as baron of Manchester. Baron Nigel would retain this office through to his death on 1086, despite De Poitou regaining control of his lands with the succession of William Rufus.

Nigel's successor was his son-in-law, Albert de Gresle (or Grelley). The Grelley family originated from Lincolnshire, although they also held lands in Norfolk, Suffolk and Nottinghamshire. Also, as well as the barony of Manchester, Albert had also been award part of the Honour of Blackburnshire by De Poitou, and would retain this through to De Poitou's final exile in 1102, for plotting against Henry I. Later, the Grelley family gained more lands in the hundreds of West Derby, Leyland and Salford. It would appear, by all accounts, that, unlike many medieval families, the Grelleys proved rather adept at retaining their lands and status through out the turmoil of the medieval period. As barons of Manchester they would retain the title and lands into the fourteenth century, only losing it through a mixed combination of lack of heirs and marriage.

Although the Grelley family were now barons of Manchester, the first four barons never actually lived there, preferring instead their estate in Lincolnshire. Albert Grelley died in 1115, and was succeeded by his son Robert Grelley, whose barony was pretty uneventful and was eventually succeeded by his son Albert.

This, the third baron of Manchester, and the second to be named Albert, later married Maud, elder daughter of William Fitznigel, Constable of Chester, which raised his status quite considerably. However, despite his rising influence, Albert did not rule Manchester for long. He was well into middle-age when he gained the title from his father, and it is thought he died in around 1166.

His successor was his son, who, following almost family tradition by this time was yet another Albert. And, just like his father, only held the barony for about ten or twelve years prior to his sudden death. In fact, so unexpected was his demise that his successor, as the fifth baron, was his son, Robert, an infant of around seven years. For the years that Robert was a minor, then, the barony was controlled by his uncle, Gilbert Bassett. Robert Grelley, the fifth baron, was by far the most significant of the family, for although he had been brought up on the family's Lincoln estate, where he actually founded a Cistercian Abbey, after returning from the crusades with Richard I in 1195, he would later move to live in Manchester.

He later married Margaret, niece of William Longchamps, Chancellor to King Richard. Later, Robert was present at the signing of the Magna Carta at Runnymede, 12 June 1215, by King John; in fact, Robert had been one of the barons who had persuaded the king to agree to the signing of the famous document. This act did not stand him in good favour with the king, and Robert had all of his lands sequestered, including Manchester, later that year. Thankfully, for the Grelley family, during the following year, all the former lands were returned after the death of King John and the succession to the throne of Henry III who would be king that granted Manchester the licence to hold an annual fair, in 1222, initially for just one day per year, although this was extended to three days five years later. This was an all important step in the development of the town, for in those times fairs were far more than jugglers and clowns, they meant trade: traders from throughout the country attended fairs, selling their wares, even though the licence to hold a fair was not the same as holding a market, trade occurred, albeit illegally.

Robert Grelley died just three years after the town's fair had been extended. His successor, as the sixth baron of Manchester was his son, Thomas. However, within two years he was dead and his successor was his young son, Robert, who was about three years of age. The heir to the barony being so young meant that he was made a ward of the king, and the administration of the barony controlled by his stepmother Christina Grelley; a post she retained until 1275, when Robert became of age.

Robert's term of office as baron of Manchester began with him serving the king in his battles with the Welsh. He later married the daughter of John de Burgh, son of the former Regent, and together they had a son, named Thomas. However, fate had a hand to play in the succession of the next baron, for Robert died in 1282, just seven years after gaining the barony, and his successor was his young son, Thomas. Once more, the baron was a minor, and once more made a ward of the king. In his absence, the king placed Walter de Langton in control of the barony, a position he retained until 1299.

Once Thomas was old enough to be baron of Manchester in his own right, he was also old enough to fight for king and country, in this case against the troublesome Scots: first against the rebel William Wallace, and later on, against Robert the Bruce.

Although Manchester had been granted the right to hold an annual fair in 1222, it had been denied the right to hold an official market. Finally, in 1301, Thomas, the eighth baron, secured this right. A weekly market was awarded to Manchester in that year by the king. By this time, the town was growing rapidly, further burgesses were granted and more streets built. It had already acquired control of the surrounding manors, including Ashton under Lyne, Crumpsall and Openshaw. The annual fair and weekly market were both held in a field cleared specifically for the task, called Acresfield and it was one of the first designated sites for trading in the entire region; this later developed into St Ann's Square, following the building of St Ann's Church by Lady Ann Bland in 1708.

After the death of Thomas Grelley in 1313, without an heir to succeed him, the control of the barony passed to his sister, Joan, who married Sir John La Warre. And, although medieval Manchester would undoubtedly prosper greatly under the administration of the La Warres, initially it would have to endure some local difficulties with the popular Banastre Revolt of 1315.

At this time the county of Lancashire was administered by Thomas, Earl of Lancaster, who, like other people with power, had his favourites; in Thomas's case, it was Robert de Holland. De Holland used this favour to weld power locally, to the great annoyance of other local barons. In the September of 1315, Sir Adam Banastre, baron of Shevington, rose up against de Holland, and with other like-minded supporters – including Sir William Bradshaigh of Haigh, and Sir Henry Lea of Lea, led a rebellion. They caused havoc in the county, attacking Liverpool, Warrington, Halton Castle, near Runcorn and also Clitheroe Castle. By the end of October, they turned their attention to Manchester, attacking the home of the De Trafford family en route. At Manchester they caused death and destruction on a significant scale. Following an attack upon Preston, the authorities finally reacted to this growing rebellion. A force of some considerable size, ironically lead by De Holland and Sir Edmund de Neville, sheriff of Lancaster, engaged the rebels on the outskirts of Preston. Banastre was captured and later executed.

This rebellion was just one of the hardships that the people would have to endure during the first half of the fourteenth century. It was

*St Ann's Square in the latter part of the nineteenth century. During the medieval period, however, this area was open ground, known as Acresfield, where the annual fair and weekly market were both held. It only developed into St Ann's Square, following the building of St Ann's Church by Lady Ann Bland in 1708.*
Author's collection

a hard time for all concerned, poor harvests had lead to much of the population nearing starvation, and then there was the arrival of the Black Death, which swept across the country, almost halving the population in its wake. For the residents of Manchester, they had to endure this without the leadership and guidance of their lord and master, for Sir John had died in 1347, and had been succeeded by his grandson, Roger, who chose to remain away from the town.

In spite of his absence, Roger would have difficulty with his barony. For in 1359, Henry, Earl of Lancaster, questioned the validity of Manchester being a borough, and called for a judicial enquiry. The verdict was not in Manchester's favour, regarding it as merely a market town – albeit the biggest in the region at that time – and not a borough. This decision would place the town behind neighbours such as Preston, Liverpool, Lancaster, Wigan and even Newton; and Manchester would have to wait until 1838 before becoming a borough once more.

Following the death of Roger de la Warre in 1370, the barony passed to his son John for a short period, before it was inherited by his brother, Thomas, who apart from now being baron, was also a priest and was appointed rector to St Mary's, Manchester parish church.

The church itself held great local importance, as its neighbour Salford had no church of its own. Further importance was gained for the church in 1421, when the town was granted a royal licence to establish a College of the Clergy. The La Warres donated their former manor house to the Collegiate Church for its use as a college for the priests and as a vicarage (much later, this site would be purchased and Chetham's School, Hospital and Library were built upon it). John Huntington was appointed as the first church warden here. Soon after the main thoroughfare through the town of Manchester was renamed Deansgate, as it passed the residence of the Collegiate Church.

In 1427, the control of the barony passed through marriage from the La Warres to the West family. During the early years of their control, the West family paid little or no attention to Manchester, as they were actively involved in the Wars of the Roses. Thomas West had fought gallantly during the long and turbulent years of the Wars of the Roses, and had witnessed victory over the Yorkist king Richard III, after supporting young Henry Tudor at Bosworth. Two years later, he led the army of his king against the defiant Cornish men on Blackheath and witnessed victory once more. In later years, under the reign of Henry VIII, he took part in the Cloth of Gold. Thomas had been a close and loyal friend of Henry Tudor, and while King Henry was in Lancashire, visiting his mother and stepfather, Thomas Stanley, Earl of Derby, he stayed a while at the home of Thomas West.

Derby's first son, James Stanley, from his earlier marriage to Margaret Neville, was appointed Warden of the Collegiate Church of Manchester in 1485 (he replaced his uncle, also named James, who had held the position of warden here since 1481 to his death four years later). There had been objections to this appointment from some quarters, feeling that it was founded more on family influence than academic qualifications. Nevertheless, during his time here, James Stanley did a great deal of good work for the church: employing the services of Richard Bexwicke, from France, to produce the lavish carved choir stalls; James also had the chantry, chapels and chapter house built too. In 1509, he was made Bishop of Ely although by the time of his death in 1525, he had been excommunicated. He is buried in the Stanley chapel.

During the Tudor years, Manchester continued to grow in stature. In 1506, following the death of Hugh Oldham, Bishop of Exeter (and Chancellor to Countess Derby – who had been born in Manchester), he left sufficient funds available to create the Free Grammar School, founded in the Bexwickes Chantry. During the reign of Henry VIII, and his dissolution of the monastic houses of England, the Collegiate

*Manchester Cathedral, during a moonlit evening at the turn of the twentieth century. However, the cathedral's origins date from the creation of the parish church of St Mary founded by the fifth baron, Robert Grelley. In 1421, it became the College of the Clergy under the De La Warres.* Author's collection

*'The Oldest House in Manchester' depicting a scene on Long Millgate in 1920. Today this is a back street in modern Manchester, however, this was very different during the medieval period, when it was perhaps the main thoroughfare for the town.* Author's collection

The Oldest House in Manchester

church in the town was not dissolved. However, later, during the reign of Edward IV, it was significantly reduced in status, to that of a mere vicarage, despite the protests of the locals. In later years, however, this unpopular decision was reversed, and the powers of the church fully restored: John Dee, appointed church warden between 1596-1608, he later became an advisor to Elizabeth I. The first Court Leet was established in 1552, which controlled the day-to-day running of the town, handing out both permissions and punishments where necessary. The Earl of Derby was appointed to oversee the affairs of the Court Leet which, through the years, contained members of many prominent families in the area.

Thomas West died in 1553, leaving no children. However, in the latter years of his life, he had designated his nephew, William, to be his heir. Following his death, however, William was accused by Lord La Warre of poisoning his uncle in an effort to gain the barony that much earlier. The matter was raised before Parliament, and would be investigated at some length. The matter wrangled on, preventing William from taking up the post of Baron of Manchester for some years; in the end, though, the matter was resolved, no evidence could be found to suggest that foul play was involved, and William served as baron until his death in 1570. Once again, just like his uncle before him, he left no heir. The succession eventually passed to a distant relation by the name of Sir Thomas West, who became the eighteenth and last of the family to retain the barony of Manchester; though he sold the office within a decade to John Lacy, a clothier from London. Lacy retained the barony of Manchester through to 1596, when he too sold it, this time to Sir Nicholas Mosley, Lord Mayor of London.

During the troubled reign of Elizabeth I, many of the good men of Manchester fought for their Queen, many prepared to take part in battle against the Spanish Armada in 1588. By the end of the Tudor years the population of Manchester had expanded rapidly to around 5000. Already the spinning of yarn and the manufacture of textiles had begun, that in later years it would bring growth and prosperity to the town. Woollens were the prime source of manufacture in the early days, although linen was produced soon after. Imports from Ireland and other places produced further trade, and the first cotton was produced with the arrival of fustian cloth. All of this would continue to expand further, and as Manchester's fame and fortune was beginning to take shape, troubled times lay ahead.

## 2      *I*N TIMES OF TROUBLE

T HE prosperity of Elizabethan Manchester would be shattered over the next one-and-a-half centuries. With the Succession of the Stuarts, and resulting Civil War and Jacobite Rebellions, death and destruction would be inflicted upon Manchester and the nation as a whole.

### Stuart Manchester

The first step came with the death of Elizabeth I in 1603, and the choice of James Stuart, son of Mary, Queen of Scots, as king. Prior to the death of the Queen, Catholics, who had been persecuted during the latter years of her reign, had met with James and sought assurances of greater freedom. James, it seems, had played a political game, going along with their requests, only to change his mind once he gained the English throne. This betrayal caused great anger amongst the Catholic families, who were now suffering persecution equal to that they had received during the Elizabethan years. Their displeasure was to manifest itself graphically in the Gunpowder Plot in 1605, led by Catesby and Fawkes.

The Plot was to have consequences for all Catholics – even as far afield as the remote region of the North-West. Sir John Radcliffe of Ordsall Hall, near Salford, was a prominent Catholic and, although not one of the named co-conspirators in the Plot, supported their ideals. Fawkes and Catesby are said to have visited the hall to discuss the planned assassination of the King and his ministers. And later, with the plot discovered, Fawkes arrested, and Catesby and the other plotters on the run, things looked bleak for the people that had supported this reckless act. However, when the soldiers came to arrest Sir John, it is claimed that he evaded capture by leaving the hall through a secret underground passageway that emerged at the *Seven Stars Inn*.

Of course, the rejection of the Stuarts was limited to a minority, and there were many others throughout the country that supported the reign of the new royal family. Within Lancashire, this support included many of the prominent families, such as the Stanleys, Hoghtons, Irelands and Tyldesleys, to name but a few. The acceptance of King James I was never more apparent than when he passed through the county in 1617 (after returning from his one and only visit to his native Scotland), staying at the homes of many of these families, including Hoghton Tower near the River Ribble; where, its claimed he was so satisfied by the feast he received that he knighted the joint of beef, saying 'arise Sir Loin'. During his travel across the county, he spent a couple of evenings in Manchester.

Throughout his twenty-five year reign of England, King James brought both stability and prosperity to the county and gained the respect of the people. However, further trouble was to arise in the reign of the Stuarts, when James I was succeeded by his son, Charles in 1625. His reign was a deeply troubled one, and his disregard for parliament (refusing to hold one for twelve years) and his overwhelming belief in the 'divine right of kings', led ultimately to the English Civil Wars and his execution in London in 1649. Manchester, like so many other towns throughout England, saw action during the years of conflict; in fact the first experience of trouble occurred before war had officially been declared.

The Earl of Derby, the most prominent man in the whole of Lancashire, and leader of the king's forces in times of trouble, had, some years earlier, set up batteries of munitions in key north west towns, to be used in the event of war or invasion, which included towns, such as Lancaster, Preston, Liverpool, and of course, Manchester.

When difficulties arose between Parliament and the monarchy, King Charles gave orders for the gunpowder housed in the Collegiate Church of Manchester to be seized for the crown; two cavaliers, Sir Alexander Radcliffe and Thomas Prestwich, were despatched to Manchester's town centre to retrieve the ten barrels of gunpowder. On a summer's day in 1642, they rode through the streets and along Deansgate, to the priest's College, where they were openly jeered by the crowd that had gathered to herald their arrival: news of their plan had reached the town early – even though war had not started, the Salford Hundred (which included Manchester) had already declared in favour of Parliament (along with the Blackburn Hundred). The two men suffered the hostile crowd and finally reached the priests' College only to discover that the gunpowder had already gone, taken by the inhabitants. This was the first of several small victories that the people of Manchester would have over the Royalists.

Following this early success, the inhabitants rallied in further support of Parliament, behind the leadership of the church warden, Richard Heyrick. The town, which was still very small and consisted of just a handful of streets, all of which dated from the medieval period, was made ready for trouble: barricades were erected across the main streets and the locals, including those from surrounding districts, were formed into a local militia of some 5,000 men, armed with pikes and muskets.

King Charles ordered that the gunpowder should be seized from the militants of Manchester, hopefully by persuasion, or by force if necessary. In such a situation, the monarch would have turned to the assistance of his chief supporter in the region, the Earl of Derby; but in his current situation, that simply wasn't possible: William Stanley, the sixth Earl, was by now, a frail old man, who had retired to Bidston Hall on the Wirral, just one of the many properties owned by the Stanley family. His son and heir, James Stanley, Lord Strange, had taken on the role of his father – and so it was to him that the king turned too. James Stanley and Charles Stuart were actually old friends; James and his wife had dined with Charles and Henrietta Maria, on many occasions, both before and after he was king. James Stanley was a capable man, he had been Mayor of Liverpool in 1625, and was married the following year to Charlotte de La Tremiolle, in the Hague on the 26 June. She was the daughter of Earl Claude Duc de Thours, the granddaughter of the Dutch King, William I, Prince of Orange. Through their years of marriage they would have no less than nine children.

**The Siege of Manchester**
Lord Strange took up the king's challenge and set about gathering a force of around 1000 men at his headquarters in Warrington. The Royalists departed their camp on 24 September, lead by Stanley, who was supported by his close friends Sir John Girlington of Thurston Hall, South Lonsdale, who was then the High Sheriff of Lancashire, and Lord Molyneux, for the slow overnight trek to Manchester.

As they neared the outskirts of the town, they saw for the first time the defences and armed militia awaiting them. Lord Strange, reluctant to fight the inhabitants of the town, instead engaged the leaders of Manchester in discussions, pointing out that he did not want to have to resort to force, and that it was best for all concerned, if the gunpowder was given to a third party, such as the local magistrate. In spite of this softly-softly approach, the people of Manchester flatly refused to agree to his requests. With such a forthright rebuttal, it was evident to Stanley that his small, inadequate force was clearly no match for the opposition, and therefore, he had little option but to withdraw.

Throughout the days of the Manchester Siege, the parliamentarian troops were stationed on the towns streets, ready to repel any assault. Two of the town's oldest streets, including Market Street (previously Market Steade Street) and King Street: these two photographs depict those famous streets, though during the latter years of the nineteenth century. Author's collection

With yet another victory won over the Royalists, Manchester realised that a greater force was surely to return to challenge them at some point, and so they engaged the talents of Colonel Rosworm. He was a German military engineer, whose abilities had been brought to the attention of both sides. King Charles had tried in vain to enlist Rosworm to the Royalist cause offering generous inducements before hostilities could start. Rosworm, unlike many in the Roundheads' camp, was honest enough to point out that he – personally- had nothing against the English monarchy; but he felt that, nevertheless, he could not side with the king. Under Rosworm's expert leadership the local militia set about reinforcing the battlements. Defences were increased and made ready for attack – at this stage in the hostilities neither side would yield to the enemy.

Even with all of this going on, there were people within Manchester that had sympathies with the Crown, and felt that surely some sort of deal could still be struck between the two sides over the control of the gunpowder. With this in mind, they invited Lord Strange to a banquet, held in his honour, where they would guarantee his safety. They wished to offer him the solution where the merchants of the town were prepared to purchase the gunpowder, and offer him and the king a fair price in exchange for peace; the money could of course pay for further munitions elsewhere. Although James Stanley was surprised at the invitation, he knew that there were some Royalist supporters within Manchester, and felt that their offer was sincere, and so agreed to the meeting; accompanying him were Sir John Girlington and Lord Molyneux.

They received a warm and seemingly genuine welcome when they arrived in the town, flowers were scattered over the roadway and several bonfires were lit in their honour. The banquet itself was a grand affair, with no expense spared, and the three guests enjoyed the hospitality of their hosts. All was going well when Sir John received word that a hostile force was gathering in the streets outside, lead by John Holcroft. The three men fled the banqueting hall, and managed to escape into the darkness of the night unharmed.

Following this most luckiest of escapes, Lord Strange gathered an even greater force at Warrington, together with artillery, and this time supported by his old friend, Sir Thomas Tyldesley, who joined him from the Fylde with more troops and munitions, returned to Manchester to lay siege.

They attacked Manchester from two fronts; a main force from

the south – who used Alport Lodge, the home of Edward Mosley as a base and the second battery came from Salford, crossing the River Irwell at Salford Bridge. The Manchester parliamentarians had the advantage of the higher ground, and the defensive position from behind Rosworm's barricades, with Rosworm himself stationed at Salford Bridge, Captain Bradshaw on Deansgate, Captain Booth Millgate, Lieutenant Barwick at Hunt's Bank, and Captain Radcliffe stationed in the town centre, on Market Stead Lane.

Even in these times of civil war, the correct and formal approach to battle had to be observed: Lord Strange approached the barricades, and stated that he wished to have unobstructed access to the town, so his army could march through; the people of Manchester refused. The following day, even though no fighting had as yet taken place, another demand for access was made; which was also refused.

Battle commenced, the Royalist artillery pounded the defences of the town relentlessly. Equally the rebels returned fire, although they could not match the strength of their opposition (having no artillery of their own) they still inflicted casualties on the Royalists. The fighting continued for days, during which time casualties were inflicted on both sides. The Royalists attempted to burn the town to the ground, and almost succeeded. And yet, regardless of the conflict, neither side was actually making any ground, and the fighting seemed to go on forever. Eventually Lord Strange called a cease-fire, and dispatched one of his cavaliers, Sir John Mounson, to negotiate: his request was that hostility should cease, as neither side had gained victory, and that they should be allowed to march through the town (as they had asked for originally) and should they be allowed to do this, they would promise to leave in peace.

This was refused, and so in an effort of compromise, Strange offered that if all the munitions were handed over they would leave in peace; this too was refused. Further compromise followed: first they asked for the payment of £1,000 for the value of the gunpowder; then it was 400 muskets; and later the figure was reduced to just forty muskets – each time the answer to the demands or requests was no; until the rebels finally told Stanley (who, by now was the seventh Earl of Derby, having received word that his father had died) that they would not be prepared to hand over not one single rusty old dagger.

The fighting resumed, if anything, far worse than before. But by now the Royalists were running extremely low on munitions, and the fighting could not be allowed to continue for much longer. So the following day, when one of his officers, a Captain Standish, was killed during an attack, the Earl used this as sufficient reason to call a withdrawal of his forces. The people of Manchester rejoiced at the retreating Royalists; they had won their first official victory of the Civil War.

The victory for the Parliamentarians at Manchester was a significant one, for although Manchester never saw fighting in its streets again during the conflict (unlike its neighbour, Liverpool, who endured three long and bloody sieges, changing from one side to another), it played an important role, as a strategic base from which to orchestrate the course of the war fought in Lancashire: the local militia who had defended the town became the Manchester Regiment, who suffered defeat at Wigan, though were victorious at Chowbent. Later, Sir Thomas Fairfax located his army at Manchester, and freed the besieged town of Nantwich with a force led from here.

### In the Aftermath of War

Before the end of the Civil War, another killer was to visit the people of Manchester – the plague. This most virulent of diseases resulted in the deaths of more than one thousand of the town's inhabitants in that one year. Matters were made all the worse with the deprivation that had resulted from the wars. The conflict had starved Manchester of trade, which led to the actual starvation of its inhabitants. No revenue was coming in to purchase food, in fact, even highly placed men such as John Rosworm went without. Eventually, following much protest, much of it lead by Rosworm complaining at not being paid for his services (which, after all had saved the town from capture), Parliament awarded the grant of £1,000, which helped to put the town back on its feet.

After the wars had ended Manchester prospered once more, in fact it was better than during the Tudor period. The market place was bustling with trade and the town continued to increase in size, more buildings were erected and further streets added. Oliver Cromwell rewarded Manchester for its loyalty to Parliament by providing its first representation in the House of Commons; the towns first MP was Charles Worsley, who had served as an officer in the New Model Army. Following his death, his successor was Richard Radcliffe, who would represent the town until his death in 1660. No more elections

*In the years immediately following the destructive civil wars, Manchester began to recover. Chetham College, created on the death of Humphrey Chetham, was a positive endorsement of this recovery. These two pictures, one modern, one older, show the changing appearance of one of Manchester's most famous landmarks.* Author's collection

took place, however, for with the Restoration in that year, Charles II deprived the town of its seat in Parliament, which would continue in fact until 1832, when the Reform Bill passed in the Commons that year allowed the election of an MP once more.

One great figure of the time was Humphrey Chetham (1580-1653). As a youngster he had been educated at Manchester Grammar School, before he acquired an apprenticeship to a linen-draper, where he gained the necessary knowledge to have confidence to go into business for himself as a clothier and woollen cloth manufacturer. His business abilities lead him to both fortune and fame, acquiring land and property; he was appointed High Sheriff of Lancashire in 1635, a position which pleased him little, as a man who disliked public attention; later when he was offered a knighthood he refused, and was fined for doing so. In the prelude to war he had been appointed the collector of the king's taxes, to gain finances to rebuild the Royal fleet; though at the outbreak of hostilities he showed favour to Parliament, allowing their forces to use his home at Turton Tower as a headquarters. Following the end of the wars, Chetham attempted to purchase the priests College in Manchester (which had been used as a prison to hold captured Royalists) but Parliament refused; it was only following his death that his will left sufficient finances to purchase the property, that Parliament agreed; it became a school in 1656, later joined by hospital and the famous Chetham Library, the first free public library in the entire country.

Towards the end of the seventeenth century Manchester was one of the most prosperous places in the region, warehouses were springing up right through the town, the woollen trade and early cotton manufacture was growing in stature, and young men of the town were gaining apprenticeships. It was also a time of religious rebellion, as nonconformist ministers were preaching in towns such as Manchester. The 1665 *Five Mile Act* was passed through Parliament to stop this occurring, forcing the ministers to the outskirts, where they continued to preach, using barns and outposts. George Fox founded the Society of Friends – better known as the Quakers – although many of their members were imprisoned for it, including Fox himself.

**Political Intrigue**
With the thoughts of the return of Catholicism as the state religion, many people were beginning to distrust the Stuarts. This lead to the bloodless revolution of 1688, when James II was opposed in favour

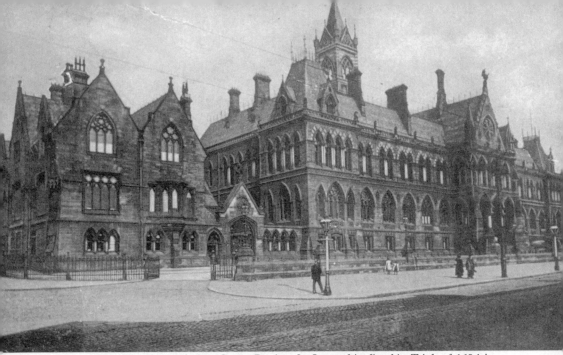

*The Manchester Assizes Court. During the Lancashire Jacobite Trials of 1694 its predecessor was the scene of great political intrigue, as crowds gathered outside to hear the verdict : would the Catholics be found guilty, or be set free? The county held its breath.* Author's collection

of William of Orange and Queen Mary. This caused uproar amongst the supporters of the Jacobite cause, throughout the country groups gathered in secret to discuss the return of James II, nowhere more so than in Lancashire. At Standish Hall, just outside Wigan, conspirators gathered, including members of many of the prominent local families, to plan both the reinstatement of the Stuart king, and the assassination of William III. Within their company was a traitor, however, John Lunt, who would later inform the authorities of the group's plan, leading to their arrest and the trial of the Lancashire Plot of 1694. The conspirators were: William Standish, Sir William Gerard, Lord Molyneux, Sir Thomas Clifton, Philip Langton, Sir Rowland Stanley and William Dicconson. The charge before them was treason, and should they be found guilty, the penalty was death. The conspirators were brought to Manchester for trial, where a surprise lay in store for the prosecution: the conspirators had been aware of the presence of Lunt and his loyalties, and had taken the precaution of not telling him their true identities, but instead had used the name of another member of the group; this was to play well for them in court. When the prosecutor called his chief witness, John Lunt, he asked him to name the men, pointing them out in the dock; each time Lunt tried to do this, he gave the wrong name of the man he was pointing at. There was uproar in the court, the defence council called for all the charges to be dropped on the grounds that the chief prosecution witness was clearly unreliable. They were all acquitted, the Judge saying 'Let me therefore say to you, go and sin no more, least a worse thing befall you'.

With the death of Queen Anne in 1714, the Elector of Hanover became king as George I. This angered the Jacobite's further and ultimately lead to the 1715 Rebellion, where James Stuart, son of the former king, James II, was hailed as the rightful monarch, as James III. Just before the start of the rebellion, trouble occurred in many North-West towns, including Warrington, Preston, Lancaster and Manchester; here a group of supporters, led by the local blacksmith, Thomas Syddall, attacked the Dissenters' Chapel in Cross Street, on the Old Pretender's birthday. The spread of this public disorder alarmed the powers-that-be, and an army was despatched to the north lead by General Wills. The trouble was soon brought under control, and eventually Syddall and his co-conspirators were arrested.

## Jacobite Rebellions

The 1715 rebellion itself, although well supported was short lived: the Scottish invading army came a cropper at Preston, defeated and humiliated by General Wills. Thomas Syddall was freed by the rebels and fought at Preston, though like many more Jacobites, he was captured and later executed. Thirty years later, and another Jacobite army invaded from Scotland, this time led by the grandson of James II, Charles Edward Stuart (Bonnie Prince Charlie to his supporters, the Young pretender to his enemies – as his father had been referred to as the Old Pretender in the last rebellion). This was the final attempt to place a Stuart on the throne once more. The Prince had landed on the shores of Scotland from his exile in France, and had raised an army of Scottish Jacobites to march on London. This was perhaps an ideal time to catch the Hanoverians off their guard, as their armies were all abroad, and the country was vulnerable to attack from within. However, despite this ideal opportunity, the Jacobites reception, from town to town, was disappointing: it was much cooler than the previous rebellion, where each town they entered they were met by hundreds of supporters ready to join their army, whereas this time round it was a mere handful.

Regardless of disappointment, they continued through Cumberland and Westmorland, into Lancashire, stopping at

*St Ann's Square, seen here on a moonlit evening during the nineteenth century, was created in 1708, in the seemingly trouble-free years prior to the two Jacobite risings, when Manchester, like other northwest towns was enjoying a period of good trade and prosperity.* Author's collection

Lancaster, before moving on to Preston where the previous attempt had failed. They progressed to Wigan, but by now the distinct lack of response to the rebellion was beginning to make the Prince feel uneasy. Perhaps they were making too swift a progress from town to town, and the news of their approach was not giving sufficient time for volunteers to join up. He gave orders to his generals that they should slow the progress of the marching army, and stop longer at the next destination; they chose the town of Manchester to call a halt.

On 29 November 1745 the first handful of rebels marched into Manchester, led by the strangest of combinations: a sergeant, a drummer boy and a young girl. Their arrival had caused a panic amongst the population. Unlike the siege of the Civil War, the people of Manchester this time did not want a fight. They hid behind their doors, or peered out of windows, unsure of the response they might expect from the rebel forces. The forward company arrived in the town by nightfall, and announced that billets were to be made available by the locals for the rebel troops. The remainder of the Jacobite army, including the Prince, arrived in Manchester the following day, having camped at Wigan the previous evening. Initially only thirty men signed up to the Jacobite cause, and even this small number admitted that they were unemployed and would have been happy to sign up to an army on either side. However, during the next couple of days, through whatever means, the Jacobites managed to raise more men to join up, bringing the total to around 300. These would form the Manchester Regiment, led by Colonel Francis Towneley, whose headquarters was the *Bulls Head Inn*.

The Jacobite army continued their progress south on 1 December, reaching Derby soon after, and were heartened to hear news that the Royal family were making plans to flee to the safety of Hanover, and that the crown jewels had already been packed (in fact, the news of the rebel army marching on London had caused a run on the pound). The jubilation of the Prince and his generals was to be short lived, for later the same day, they also received word that the Duke of Cumberland, who had been hastily recalled from Europe, was leading an army north, at speed, to intercept them. The Prince wanted to engage in battle with the Duke and eagerly awaited his arrival; only to be told that another army, lead by General Wade, was approaching from the north-east: to be caught between two armies would be military madness, so the Prince reluctantly, under advisement from his generals, agreed to retreat.

News of this forced retreat soon reached Manchester, and many of the men loyal to George II planned to give them a hostile reception on their return. This was later stopped under the direction of the local magistrates, who feared that conflict within the streets of the town would surely bring about its destruction. So the Jacobite force was allowed to enter Manchester once more unmolested; they rested here just the one night, before continuing their retreat as the Hanoverians were fast approaching. During their stay, however, they insisted that the sum of £5,000 should be handed over; the locals resisted, until hostages were seized and threatened with execution, and so the money was handed over.

The Jacobites reached Wigan by 10 December, reaching Preston by the following day, arriving in Lancaster by the 13th. They reached

*For the members of the Manchester Regiment, the '45 Jacobite Rebellion came to a bloody close at Carlisle. Many of their number were transported to London to face charges of treason in the following July: having been found guilty, they were executed, their severed heads displayed on pikes outside Manchester's Town Hall. Here we can see the modern town hall, built in 1877.* Author's collection

Carlisle by the 19th, and left the Manchester Regiment, still lead by Colonel Towneley, to hold Carlisle Castle, while the Prince and the remainder of the army fled to Scotland. The Prince promised to send reinforcements to Carlisle, but they never arrived.

By now the two Hanoverian armies had combined, and were joined by the Liverpool Blues, who converged on Carlisle: although the Manchester Regiment fought gallantly, they were completely out numbered, in the end they surrendered. Many of their number were transported to London to face charges of treason in the following July: having been found guilty, they were executed, their severed heads displayed on pikes outside Manchester's town hall.

# 3     THE CANAL AGE

T HE canal age, between 1755 -1830, made a huge leap in the efficiency of transport, and would prove to be a significant period in industrial history. For, just like the turnpikes had been an improvement over the old roads, the arterial canals would surpass the navigation's, as rather than being tied to the direction of the river, they could be cut to link places of need. In fact, canals would transform Manchester's transport infrastructure beyond all recognition – soon Manchester would be the canal capital of the North-West of England.

The arrival of the first industrial canal is of great historical significance. However, to this day, there is still great debate, between the Sankey Canal at St Helens, or the Bridgewater Canal as to which was the original English canal. It is fair to say that the Sankey was to be yet another navigation, and indeed was granted parliamentary permission as the *Sankey Brook Navigation Act*. Though, in actual fact, Henry Berry, its creator, was what we might call 'economical with the truth', and rather than attempting to navigate the Sankey Brook, cut an arterial canal instead. It is equally fair to say that the Bridgewater, begun two years after the Sankey had been completed, was the first English waterway to be constructed under a *Canal Act*, and indeed gained its relatively easy acceptance by Parliament due to the overwhelming success of the Sankey Canal.

## The Bridgewater Canal

Francis Egerton became the third Duke of Bridgewater at the age of eleven, although he was lucky to ever gain the title in the first place. His father, Scroop Egerton, the first Duke of Bridgewater, had married twice, gaining a daughter and two sons from the first marriage, and a further four sons and four daughters from the second marriage. Francis was the third youngest of these four; all the children from the first marriage died young, and so too did Charles Egerton, the first son of the second marriage. Francis's father died when he was eight, and his older brother John became the second Duke of Bridgewater. However, John died in 1748, and Francis, then just eleven, became the third Duke of Bridgewater.

Francis was a weak and sickly child, suffering tuberculosis from an early age. His mother, Lady Rachel Russell, remarried soon after the

Prior to the arrival of the Bridgewater Canal, the Mersey & Irwell Navigation was the main link between the cotton warehouses of Manchester and the port of Liverpool. This illustration (above) depicts the navigation at Ordsall; note the amount of factories located alongside this main transport medium. Whereas the more recent photograph (below) shows the Irwell now in more tranquil times. H E Tidmarsh/Author's collection

death of the first husband, to Sir Richard Lyttleton, a man who was considerably her junior. It would appear that young Francis was regarded as being slow, even retarded, and considered an embarrassment to the family, and was packed off to boarding school, later gaining a place at Eton. It had been rumoured, amongst family and friends, that if Francis had not bucked up his ideas, he would have lost his inheritance, as it could have been awarded to another member of the family.

It was a popular practice amongst the landed gentry to allow their children to attend the Grand Tour of Europe, whereby they could travel and gain a wider education. Francis attend the tour, along with his tutor and early mentor, Robert Wood. On his travels he would have witnessed the canals of Europe, in particular the Languedoc Canal in France.

On his return to England, now a young man, Francis was attracted by the bright lights and excitement of the society scene of London and Newmarket, which included excessive drinking and gambling. It was here that he met and fell in love with Elizabeth Gunning, the Duchess of Hamilton, a young widow. It was her rejection to Francis's proposal of marriage that significantly altered his life. Broken-hearted, Francis retreated from society back to his estates at Worsley, becoming something of an eccentric, not washing or changing his clothes for weeks on end.

During his absence, his estates had been managed by his sister, and her husband Lord Stafford. They had employed the talents of John Gilbert, as estates manager; which included the running of the coal mines on the estate too. He had gained the position as his brother, Thomas Gilbert was General Land Agent to both the Bridgewater Estate and the Duke's brother-in-law, Lord Gower. It is claimed that when the two men met, on the Duke's return to Worsley in 1757, they immediately became close friends.

John Gilbert was a qualified engineer, he had served an apprenticeship at Boultons of Birmingham – one half of the design team that invented the much acclaimed Boulton & Watt engine. Although the coal mines at Worsley were productive, they, like many other early mines, were a victim of flooding which reduced the output of coal. An attempt had been made to reduce the amount of water in the mines, which in some cases came from almost six hundred feet below the surface, with the cutting of a slough into the hillside, years before, which had only been partly successful as it was cut too close to the surface was prone to collapse. Gilbert used his engineering knowledge to remedy this, by cutting a new slough, wider and deeper than before and at a steeper angle, which proved successful. The slough was in fact large enough to float barges along it (known as starvation boats, as they were so thin), which were propelled to the surface by colliers lying on their backs, strapped to the boats, pushing them along with their feet used to transport the coal to the surface, which was quicker than using the conventional winding gear. In 1797, the famous Incline Plane was built, which brought the boats to the surface by the force of water, for which the Duke was awarded the Gold Medal of the Society of Arts.

Such was the amount of water feeding from the slough, that Gilbert suggested to the Duke that it could be used to feed an artificial waterway, that could be used to transport their coal wherever they required. Since the success of the Sankey Canal, completed in 1757, Parliament had warmed to the idea of creating these artificial waterways. Previously the Duke had used the turnpikes and the Mersey & Irwell Navigation to transport his coal to Manchester, both of which were wholly unreliable and expensive; the idea of his own canal impressed the Duke, knowing he could substantially reduce the cost of coal.

Turnpikes had been slow to arrive at Manchester, compared with other parts of the county: since the first turnpike opened in 1726, between Liverpool and Prescot, followed in the same year by another between Prescot and Warrington, it would be 1735 before the Manchester-Oldham turnpike opened; followed by others to Rochdale and Bury in 1755.

A Bill was presented to Parliament, to build the canal – known as the Worsley Canal – in December 1758, by Henry Tomkinson, a Manchester solicitor, aided by John Gilbert, who was called upon to give evidence regarding the engineering required to build such an arterial canal. The *Worsley Canal Act* was given Royal Assent on 23 March 1759, the first of its type, for the construction of a still water canal, not a navigation. Previous to this, fearing that Parliament might reject the idea of a canal, a second option, of using the Worsley Brook at a tool for navigation, had been considered, but following the success of the bill, was dropped. This first Act only allowed the construction of the canal between Worsley and Salford, as the original intended destination was Ordsall Hall. But later the Duke would change his mind. Nevertheless, construction of the famous canal began later in 1759, and would take four years to complete the original section, with hundreds of Irish navvies employed, many of which had worked in the Sankey Canal, to dig the channel by hand, using pick and shovel.

For the actual building of the canal, the Duke realised there would be so much work involved that apart from himself and Gilbert, a third engineer would be needed, and instructed Gilbert to seek a like minded engineer: this was to be James Brindley (1716-1772) a man who had gained a notable reputation in the use of water as an engineering tool.

James Brindley was born in a tiny thatched cottage in the Derbyshire village of Tunstead, within the parish of Wormhill, on the outskirts of Buxton. The son of a poor family, his father was a farm labourer, and a man regarded locally as something of a waster. Tunstead's link to James Brindley is still celebrated to this day, and although the family cottage no longer exists, a sign marks the spot in the village where it once stood. James gained an apprenticeship in 1733, with Abraham Bennett, a wheelwright of Sutton near Macclesfield. His old workshop still stands to this day, although modernised through the years, a plaque on the wall confirms that this was where Brindley served his apprenticeship. Although it was a humble start, Brindley would prove to be the best worker that Bennett ever employed, showing a natural aptitude for engineering and problem solving with the use of practical mechanics in later years Brindley managed the business through to his master's death in 1742. Later that same year, Brindley relocated to Leek, setting up his own, small business, which must have prospered, for eight years later he was renting further premises, at Burslem, Staffordshire, from the Wedgwoods.

Brindley was illiterate, and would sketch out his plans in chalk on the floor – though it was common, in those days, and even in the following century, to have engineers who could neither read nor write, as they learned their skill through practical experience. However, Brindley's temperament was that should a problem be encountered that could not immediately be solved, it would bother him greatly and he would take to his bed, staying there for days if necessary, until the solution presented itself. Nevertheless, his abilities as an engineer shone through, and he gained the greatest acclaim for his work on the Wet Earth Colliery, at Clifton, in 1752. This, like many mines, suffered with severe flooding, and Brindley was asked to try and solve the problem. His unique solution was to run a long water flow, rather like a mill race, of which most was underground (even passing under the River Irwell), to build up sufficient head of water to drive a pump which pumped the mine dry. Such was the ability of this design it remained in use through to the 1950s. Three years later, he was busy working on several projects at the same time; a silk mill at Congleton; designing his own steam engine, which he patented; and perhaps most importantly, commissioned by Earl Gower and Lord Anson to survey the route of a canal to connect the rivers of the Trent and Mersey (this was the second such survey, the first had been done by the Liverpool Common Council three years earlier) which was abandoned due to cost.

Brindley was employed by the Duke to work on the Bridgewater Canal from the late summer of 1759. It is suggested that although Gilbert had hired him, the two men did not see eye-to-eye: the two men were of completely different characters. Brindley was loud and brash, and a heavy drinker, who, it is clamed, would arrive for work the following morning, still drunk, or hung-over, from the night before – which annoyed Gilbert immensely. Once Brindley had discovered success, and the wealth that went with it, these parts of his character were exaggerated further still, for apart from drinking to excess, he would also eat to excess, not leaving the dinner table until he was sure the buttons on his waistcoat were about to pop. Gilbert, on the other hand, was a more mature, level-headed and thoroughly reserved man, an eminent engineer in his own right of course, with superior intelligence to Brindley. Born in Staffordshire, the son of a quarry owner, he had gained an apprenticeship at the age of twelve with Matthew Boulton, but had to leave at nineteen, following the sudden death of his father, to return home to run the family's lime works.

Although the Duke's original intention was to take the canal through to Salford, and link to the Mersey & Irwell Navigation, on reaching the river, in July 1761, he changed his mind: after all, it had been the unreliability of the navigation that had made the idea of constructing a canal so interesting in the first place, why reduce it's efficiency by joining a poor navigation? Crossing the river presented two large problems: the passing of another Bill through Parliament, and should that be approved, the construction of an aqueduct.

The second Bill was strongly contested by the local turnpike trustees, fearful of the competition it would undoubtedly cause. Further objections came from the proprietors, annoyed that the canal was not to connect to their waterway as originally planned, fearful of the competition, but also wanted assurances that the canal would not, under any circumstances, draw water from the Irwell. During the committee stage of the second Bill, the Duke had to justify to the House of Commons in particular, that there was sufficient need for a canal to continue through to

*The Duke's decision to cross the River Irwell, rather than lock down to it, meant the building of the famous Barton Aqueduct: it stood thirty-nine feet high, and was over 200 yards in length, spanning the river over three arches. The very idea of its construction was condemned as being impossible, but James Brindley thought otherwise. However, on completion, as the water began to flow in, Brindley, once confident, now fled, forecasting disaster. The Duke along with Gilbert remained and held their breath in anticipation, crossing their fingers in the hope that it would work. It did, of course, and was described in the press of the time as being 'the greatest artificial curiosity in the world', and the first barge crossed safely on the 24 July, 1761.* H E Tidmarsh

Manchester, assisted by both Gilbert and Brindley. The benefits of such a waterway outweighed the criticisms, and the Bill was passed.

Crossing the Irwell meant the building of the famous Barton Aqueduct: it stood thirty-nine feet high, and was over 200 yards in length, spanning the river over three arches. When the public heard of the intention to create an aqueduct it was openly condemned, describing it as an impossible feat – sheer madness that one vessel could sail over another. Although Brindley designed the structure, early tests proved that it was unsound, and had to be altered by Gilbert. The channel was first lined with straw and topped with a

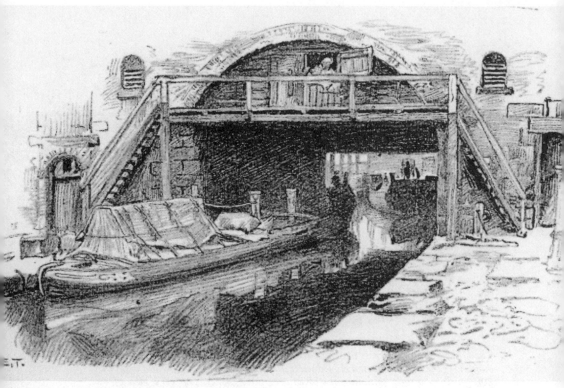

*The Bridgewater Canal reached Castlefield in 1765. The canal's arrival heralded the creation of a transport hub, with the building of many warehouses, and a huge coal wharf, making the area a hive of activity. Tidmarsh has attempted to capture some of this activity in his illustration.* H E Tidmarsh

thick layer of clay to prevent the water seeping through. During the time it was ready to be connected to the canal, onlookers watched in amazement, wondering if the stone structure would crack under the immense strain. As the water flowed in, all those present, including the Duke and Gilbert (Brindley had fled, forecasting disaster) held their breath in anticipation, and crossed their fingers, hoping it would work. It did, of course, and was described in the press of the time as being 'the greatest artificial curiosity in the world', opening for passage on 24 July 1761.

With this success, the canal continued towards Manchester, although it had to cross the notorious Trafford Moss, a wet and boggy area – this was achieved by draining the streams and laying hardcore. A further Bill, seeking permission to take a section of canal into Cheshire, through to Runcorn – in order to create a

*These two images of Castlefield — Tidmarsh's drawing of the nineteenth century view, and the photograph taken in 2002 — offer a stark contrast of the same scene, from industrial to leisure.* H E Tidmarsh/The Author

*Following the decline of the canals in favour of the faster railways, Castlefield suffered a prolonged period of dereliction. However, in more recent years the canal network has suddenly become popular once more and Castlefield has witnessed a rejuvenation, combining business, residential and leisure activities - as these three photographs show.* The Author

Although much has been done at Castlefield, the task is still very much on-going.
The upper picture shows one of the former warehouses, located just off from the
Bridgewater Canal, in a stage of rebuilding - while the second (below) depicts a
warehouse located alongside the Rochdale Canal, still derelict and desperately in
need of restoration. The Author

*The Duke's decision to take the canal through to Runcorn was given parliamentary permission in March 1762. However, to take the canal into Cheshire was a huge engineering task, and this, along with opposition from the Brookes family of Norton Priory, delayed its completion until 1776. This photograph shows the canal in the 1950s passing through Stretford.* The Author

reliable link to the sea – was passed by Parliament in March 1762. The main section of canal reached Pomona in 1763, and Castlefield, Manchester in 1765. The arrival of the canal at Castlefield was heralded with the building of many warehouses, originally in timber, but later rebuilt in brick during the nineteenth century. But the main trade at Castlefield was coal, as the canal halved the cost, and the huge Castlefield Coal Wharf opened in 1765.

To take the canal into Cheshire was a huge engineering task, it meant the building of another aqueduct over the River Mersey, the crossing of the Stretford meadows, using a 900 yard long embankment, standing seventeen feet high and one hundred feet wide; and another huge embankment to cross the Bollin Valley, built in 1767. As the canal neared Runcorn, the Duke faced stiff opposition from the Brookes family of Norton Priory, who objected to the canal crossing their estate. Although this problem was rectified, it delayed the canal's completion at Runcorn until 1776.

In total, from the mines at Worsley, through to both Manchester and Runcorn, covering a total of forty-two miles, the Bridgewater is a contour canal, remaining at eighty-five feet above sea level throughout, eliminating the need for locks. The total cost was to reach £200,000, and the Duke had been forced to borrow heavily from London bankers, friends and family, and sold much of the land and property he owned in order for it to succeed – in fact, it almost bankrupted him, and he was an old man before he finally cleared all of his loans.

**The Birth of Canal Mania**
James Brindley had made his fame for canal building with the Bridgewater, doubtless due to his abilities, but also for he was the engineer who was out in front. While both the Duke and Gilbert were busy, going over what Brindley had done, making sure everything was up to scratch (and when it wasn't rectifying it), they had little time for chatting to onlookers or the press, whereas Brindley was only too happy to stop and talk. But to be fair, it was Brindley, of the three men who gained the most, gaining the title 'father of the canals'. And would go on to play an active role in many of the canals that followed.

A collaboration between the Duke and Josiah Wedgewood, lead to the connection of the Bridgewater to the Trent & Mersey Canal (originally called the Grand Trunk Canal), with Brindley as the chief engineer, work began on 26 July 1766. Bridgewater's waterway joined with the Leeds & Liverpool Canal at Leigh in 1800. Following this connection, the Duke placed a fourth Bill before Parliament, to extend the canal from Castlefield through to Stockport, but his plans were rejected.

Within a year of beginning the construction of the Trent & Mersey Canal, Brindley was in failing health, brought on by his diabetes and overwork. Although he had had a long term relationship with Mary

The Rochdale Canal, which opened in 1804, was the first of the trans-Pennine
canals. The link with Yorkshire was deemed vital to the growth in the textile trade.
Tidmarsh's illustration of the canal during its heyday of the nineteenth century
offers us an insight into the activity that once occurred on Manchester's canals –
whereas the two modern photographs show the same canal peaceful and tranquil,
seemingly the ideal place to go. H E Tidmarsh/The Author

Bennett – and they had a son, John, born August 1759 – Brindley later married, at the age of forty-nine, Anne Henshall (the daughter of John Henshall the land surveyor), who was just eighteen, in 1765. The couple lived at Turnhurst Hall, in Newchapel, Staffordshire; they had two daughters, Susannah and Anne. Brindley died, 30 September 1772, and was buried in St James' Church, Newchapel. The Trent & Mersey Canal was completed by Brindley's brother-in-law, Hugh Henshall.

Francis Egerton died in 1804, his estate and canal were controlled by trustees. He, along with fellow engineers, Gilbert and Brindley, had created the first true canal, and indeed the canal age. In the wake of this followed a 'canal building mania' that fuelled the expansion of the new industrial society. Certainly, around Manchester, other canals were planned and created.

The Manchester, Bolton and Bury Canal had been discussed since the mid 1780s, although it was only surveyed in 1790, by Matthew Fletcher, a leading coal proprietor in the Irwell Valley. Fletcher employed the services of Hugh Henshall, brother-in-law of James Brindley, to conduct a professional survey in the following year. Such was the liking for canals that Parliament passed the Bill for its construction later, in May 1791. Surprisingly, Henshall was not chosen as the chief engineer, instead John Nightingale, Fletcher's nephew, was given the post. Although the canal was relatively short, at just sixteen miles, its difficult terrain meant that it required no less than seventeen locks and three stone aqueducts. Water for the canal was supplied by Fletcher's Wet Earth Colliery, at Clifton, together with a reservoir built at Summerseat. Apart from the terminus at Manchester, this canal had two other wharves, one at Bolton and another at Bury, both of which were completed by 1794. Although the canal had been built with the primary concern of transporting coal, later passenger traffic formed an increasingly large proportion of the canal's trade.

To run the new canal, a company was formed, trading as the Manchester, Bolton & Bury Canal and Navigation Company, consisting of its leading shareholders, which included the Earl's of Derby and Wilton. Such was the success of the canal that in 1801, plans were announced to extended it, via an aqueduct over the River Irwell, to link it to the Rochdale Canal. This was a rather over-ambitious plan and was later dropped due to cost.

By 1831, with the railway era in its infancy, the proprietors of the Manchester, Bolton & Bury Canal gained the necessary parliamentary approval to create a railway of their own – changing their trading name to the Manchester, Bolton & Bury Canal, Navigation & Railway Company in the process. For a time, it was rumoured that the canal was to be filled in and the railway built over it, however, due to complaints from the services that used the canal, this was altered, and the railway was instead built along side, opening in 1838. In 1846, it amalgamated with the Manchester & Leeds Railway Company, who in turn, were taken over by London, Midland and Scottish Railway.

Despite the addition of the railway, the canal continued to operate with some success. However, it suffered a vast breach in July 1936, at Prestolee, so severe that the cost of repair was far beyond its commercial value, so it was filled in. The canal, now in two halves, continued in use, mainly for coal transportation along the Irwell Valley, until its complete closure in the mid 1940s.

Other canals were started, or suggested. The idea of constructing a Leigh, Wigan and Salford Canal was mentioned for a time, though like many projected canal proposals, it faded away without trace. In June 1792, plans were passed to construct another canal from Manchester, initially called the Ashton under Lyne & Oldham Canal, it was later shortened to the Ashton Canal. The Ashton Canal commenced construction in 1794, heading east it linked with the Huddersfield Canal, which had begun in the same year. The Ashton Canal had sections open for use within two years, although was only fully operational in 1800; whereas the Huddersfield Canal, constructed by Sir Edward Pinkerton, only opened in 1811, having been unavoidably delayed by the construction of what was to become the longest canal tunnel – at over four miles – ever seen in the country, at Standedge. Once completed, the Huddersfield Canal was linked to the Calder & Hebble Navigation, via the Huddersfield Broad Canal ( designed by Sir John Ramsden) and connected to the Peak Forest Canal at Dukkenfield. This connection formed one of the three trans-Pennine canals.

A canal network linking Lancashire to Yorkshire was deemed vital to the cotton industry, and had been a priority for a number of years with several routes planned. In fact, the race to cross the Pennines lead to the first being last and the last becoming the first. For although the Leeds & Liverpool Canal was the first of the three trans-Pennine canals to be commenced, it would actually be the last to be completed, due to endless delays. And the last to begin construction, the Rochdale Canal, would be the first to open to traffic!

The idea of the Rochdale Canal had first been mentioned at a meeting of interested parties, headed by Richard Townley, held in the *Union Flag Inn* at Rochdale, on 19 August 1766. The intention was to cut a canal to link the Mersey & Irwell Navigation with the Calder & Hebble Navigation. The group of businessmen hired James Brindley to carry out the survey early the following year, but in the end the estimated cost proved too high to continue. The idea was resurrected once more in the summer of 1790, when another group of businessmen assembled and formed a committee, this time hiring John Rennie to survey the intended route. The proposal was placed before Parliament in the spring of the following year, though was rejected following opposition from mill owners. Undeterred, the plans were altered, and put before parliament for a second time – which yet again met with rejection. A new survey was commissioned, this time carried out by William Jessop, and put back before parliament, this, the third time gaining Royal Assent in April 1794. Following its final approval by Parliament, William Jessop was given the position of chief engineer, assisted by William Crossley. Construction was swift and the waterway opened to traffic by 1804. This was by far the busiest of the three canals between Lancashire and Yorkshire.

The canal enjoys links with the Bridgewater at Castlefield, and with the Ashton Canal at London Road. Leaving Manchester, it travels to Rochdale, before continuing thirty-three miles over the moorland hills, via a total of ninety-two locks into Yorkshire, linking cotton towns like Todmorden, Hebden Bridge and Sowerby Bridge, where it links with the Calder & Hebble Navigation. Hollingworth Lake, covering 120 acres, was built specifically to feed the canal, and ensure a consistent water level throughout.

The Rochdale Canal enjoyed overwhelming success until the beginning of the railway era, when like other canals, it witnessed a reduction in trade. It was leased to the Manchester & Leeds Railway Company in 1845, and this was taken over a decade later by a consortium of four railway companies ; this had become the norm in the latter part of the nineteenth century – the Leeds and Liverpool had been taken over by three railway companies five years earlier, and the Huddersfield Canal had been bought by LNWR. The Rochdale Canal remained in operation through to 1937, although only officially closed, following an *Act of Parliament*, in 1952.

Manchester's last conventional canal was the Manchester and Salford Junction Canal, designed to connect the Rochdale Canal to the River Irwell, which passed through Parliament in July 1836, and was opened three years later. This was a strange waterway, in that from day one it was losing trade to the Bridgewater's connection to the Irwell, via the Hulme lock, so much so that within a year it had been bought out by the Mersey & Irwell Navigation Company. The canal closed after its purchase by the Cheshire Lines Committee in 1875, who filled it in soon after.

During their heyday, the Manchester canals brought great trade to Manchester and the surrounding area. They, along with the Mersey & Irwell Navigation, were the lifeline to the Port of Liverpool and the other industrial towns of Lancashire, only losing out in the end to the railways in the following century.

# 4 *K*ING COTTON

**M**ANCHESTER made its name as the capital of King Cotton in the latter part of the eighteenth century, but of course spinning and weaving had been traditional practices in Lancashire, long before the Industrial Revolution, using wool taken from the sheep grazing on the moorland hills. Cotton arrived during the seventeenth century, a more versatile material to work with, it could be woven or spun separately or even mixed with the traditional wool. Through the years the greater demand for cotton exceeded that of wool. Fustian cloth was one of the earliest, which is warp and weft.

In the early days all the spinning and weaving occurred in the home, in the cellars of the cottages. This cottage-based textile industry existed through to the eighteenth century, and in some cases beyond. It operated in two distinct forms. Clothiers would purchase wool or cotton and distribute this amongst the local spinners and hand-weavers, for it to be made into cloth. The alternative was smaller clothiers, who purchased their own wool and yarn, who would weave it themselves; once completed they could take it along to the local cloth hall where it could be sold. Both of

*In the early days, prior to the creation of mills and factories, the humble textile industry existed on the 'cottage or domestic system'. This meant families working together, normally in the damp cellars – the women spinning and the men weaving. The work, along with the raw materials, was handed out, and the completed items then taken to the local cloth hall for sale.* H E Tidmarsh

these very traditional styles operated on a homespun method, the work carried out predominantly by women and young girls.

The dramatic change, to both spinning and weaving, (though initially to spinning) occurred in the latter half of the eighteenth century, with the arrival of the factory system. Here, workers were employed by the proprietor, and paid a weekly wage for the work they did. These factories, or mills, used water power, from a specially constructed mill race to turn the waterwheel and power the looms.

These early mills were built in remote locations, amongst the hills and alongside rivers, from which they drew their water supply. But cotton not only brought employment to Lancashire, it created communities. Due to the remote locations, the mill owners had to form co-operatives that were self-sufficient, with houses and cottages for the workforce alongside the mill, plus schools, chapels and shops. Barrow Bridge, on the outskirts of Bolton, is a fine example of this working practice, which attracted the attention and praise of Prince Albert and Benjamin Disraeli. Of course, village communities such as these were not built on the basis of any charitable intent, but on sound working practice and good business sense, as it ensured the work force was always available.

**Innovations**
Through the early developing years attributed to the Industrial Revolution, a number of significant innovations occurred for the new textile industry, which ensured that the change from cottage-based domestic work, to factory production, prospered. These were major innovations that improved production and the efficiency of the operation.

John Kay, born in 1704, at Park Cottages, on the outskirts of Bury, would later gain an apprenticeship with a local loom maker, and his natural talents for the trade soon manifested themselves in a number of important inventions, such as the weft, a simple flattened metal strip which held the threads together, and in place, making the operation of weaving much smoother. However, his most famous invention, the Flying Shuttle, was introduced in 1733. This was a massive improvement in weaving terms. Traditionally, weaving was carried out on the large hand-operated looms, which required two weavers, in order to throw the shuttle back and forth. Kay's invention, using what was referred to as a 'picking stick', caused the shuttle to return to the start position at the end of the weave all by itself, which was quicker than the traditional method and, most

The arrival of the factory system revolutionised the textile industry. More goods could be made in a much quicker time, and far more people were employed – the very essence of the Industrial Revolution, at which Manchester was at the forefront. H E Tidmarsh

The spinning rooms were unhealthy places in which to work, largely due to the high level of humidity required to work the cotton. In this illustration its easy to see why places like Manchester were often referred to as 'spindle country'. Within the spinning room each operator would be responsible for the operation of around ten machines, each with around fifty spindles. H E Tidmarsh

*The large weaving sheds were largely the domain of the women. It was such a noisy environment, with the constant crashing of the looms, that the women learned to lip-read. Also, in stark contrast to the high humidity of the mills, the weaving sheds were often cold, and freezing in winter.* H E Tidmarsh

important, only required a single operator.

This new invention, which was quickly adopted by the larger weaving houses, did not go down well amongst the weavers, for obvious reasons. Riots occurred, as half the weavers were facing unemployment; they broke into Kay's home, smashing up his new device, and forcing both him, and his family, to flee the area. Although he went to live in Essex, his machine would live on in Lancashire. In the town of Bury, at the end of Market Street, in the appropriately named Kay Gardens, stands a statue of John Kay, a monument to his achievement.

The introduction of the Flying Shuttle, and the Jacquard Loom that followed it, changed the status-quo between weavers and spinners. So efficient was the new machine that the spinners were unable to match its output. However, as so often in life, when the balance had been altered heavily in one direction, something arises that swings it back again. This occurrence was the arrival of Hargreaves' Spinning Jenny.

James Hargreaves was the man that would put spinning back in step. The story that surrounds his important discovery has been told many, many times, and has taken on almost mythical proportions. His invention, it is claimed, was created quite by accident, when his young daughter, Jenny, accidentally brushed against her mother's spinning wheel, knocking it over. Hargreaves noticed that, although the spindle was now on its side, it continued to spin. The thought occurred to him that if one spindle could spin in that position, then surely several more could do the same. His machine, designed in 1765, called the Spinning Jenny, after his daughter, drove several spindles at once. It was so efficient, in fact, that it could do the work of eight spinners. In economic terms, to the mill owners, this meant that one spinner could do the work of eight, and seven were surplus to requirements.

Just like John Kay before him, Hargreaves and his family were driven out of their native Lancashire by rioting spinners, protesting that as a direct result of his invention, they were about to lose their jobs; Hargreaves and his family relocated to the Midlands. Part of the great tragedies of this was that, although his machine revolutionised spinning, making it as competitive as weaving, Hargreaves would not enjoy the benefits. For when it came to business, Hargreaves was a novice, who's gullible friendship lead to him being conned out of the patent rights of the Spinning Jenny, by so-called friends who he had actually given early prototypes of his machine to, as his invention was not patented until 1770.

Another inventor, but this time with a shrewd business brain, was Richard Arkwright. Although he was born in Preston, and lived much of his early life there (Arkwright's House, behind the parish church, still stands to this day), he later moved to Bolton, working as a barber. His greatest invention was the Water Frame, in 1769, which followed his earlier Throstle Water Frame. This device had no less that forty-eight spindles, and could now spin cotton at what must have been thought at the time an alarming rate. Arkwright had, almost all by himself, created the factory culture. The result was that he too was driven out of Lancashire, relocating to Cromford, Derbyshire and Nottingham, where he continued his work. He became a wealthy and

*Two different scenes of the Hall i' th' Wood, the home of Samuel Crompton, on the outskirts of Bolton, where he invented the Spinning Mule – a combination of Hargreaves' Spinning Jenny and Arkwright's water frame – in 1776, which helped to revolutionise the automated spinning of cotton.* Author's collection

famous businessman, later even gaining a knighthood.

Despite their advances, both Hargreaves' and Arkwright's machines tended to produce thread that was either too weak or too course; Samuel Crompton would discover a way of rectifying this situation. Crompton was born at Firwood Fold in Bolton in 1753. Later his family moved to the Hall in the Wood on the outskirts of the town, though his father, John Crompton, a tenant farmer, died soon after the move, leaving Samuel, the eldest of the children, to assist his widowed mother working the farm, as well as continuing his education. The family wove and spun cotton, especially during the long winter nights, to improve their meagre income.

So frustrated was Samuel at the continual breakage of the thread on the current machines that he set about designing his own: the Spinning Mule, a combination of the best pieces of Hargreaves' Spinning Jenny, and Arkwright's Water Frame. He was very secretive about his invention, hiding it away in a specially built place in the roof space of the hall, and blanking out all of the windows to prevent prying eyes watching him while he used it. Poverty caused him to exhibit the machine, however, for the income of mere £60; years later, Parliament recognised his achievement to the textile industry, awarding him the sum of £5,000. Nevertheless, he would die in poverty, and was buried in Bolton's parish church; local mill owners, who benefited from his invention, later collected the sum of £2,000 to erect the statue that stands in the churchyard today.

John Balderstone of Tockholes, invented the Weft Fork, a device that immediately stopped a loom the second a thread broke, thus saving thread and time. He, like Crompton, died penniless, after his friends got him drunk one night and stole both his ideas and patents. Weaving was completely transformed by an Oxford clergyman, named Edmund Cartwright, when he invented the power loom in 1785; at last weaving was automated, and by its very nature, this meant that it could be undertaken by semi-skilled workers and at speed. However, although these most radical of machines were adopted by many mills, it would be many years before the traditional hand looms were finally phased out.

Riots by textile workers were common in this time, Luddites attacked many mills, since the arrival of new machines forced them to lose their jobs. One of the worst incidents occurred at Westhoughton, in 1812, when Luddites burned down the mills, four of their leaders were arrested, tried at Lancaster, and executed, in a show of force by the authorities, and therefore demonstrating that such activities would not be permitted.

**The Age of Steam**
By the 1780s, cotton mills had spread throughout Lancashire, powered throughout by waterwheels. Yet, by the turn of the century, the industry had seen rapid changes, that would take the mills away from their remote rural villages, into the larger towns. The reason? Steam power. The first Boulton & Watt engine was installed in Manchester in 1783, and they would catch on in a big way, causing mills throughout the region to switch from water power to steam. These engines relied on coal to run, so the new mills located close to the coalfields, or at least on the canal network.

With the advent of these machines, weaving moved from the cellars of cottages into large weaving sheds, single-storey buildings, not attached to the main mill. Spinning too did the same, though a little later, in mills built to an almost identical pattern, usually five or six storeys high, although some forward looking proprietors, such as Hornby, Birley and Fielden at Blackburn, combined the two under the same roof. Mill towns were created, some concentrated on weaving, like Blackburn, Preston and Burnley; while others specialised in spinning, like Oldham, Rochdale and Bolton.

By the turn of the nineteenth century, the industry was expanding rapidly, there were now around fifty steam-powered machines employed in the textile industry within Lancashire, most of them were in Manchester itself, they powered the spinning wheels, using vertical engines with tall flywheels, and the weaving looms with horizontal engines. Manchester and Salford formed the centre for these new larger, modern mills. Manchester, and the immediate surrounding districts in the south east of the county, accounted for three quarters of the nation's cotton production: King Cotton had not only arrived, but it was here to stay. Manchester's location, nestled below the Pennines, meant that its damp climate proved ideal for spinning cotton, and the water here was soft which aided the process significantly; this, linked to the abundance of coal in the area, made it the ideal centre of the cotton trade.

Raw cotton arrived from the southern states of America, initially to the warehouses in London, situated along the Thames, but following the establishment of the Lancashire cotton industry, it switched to the North West ports, with Liverpool gaining the lion's share of this most lucrative trade. Arriving at the port of Liverpool, the raw cotton, which was stored in barrels, was unloaded on to barges which made the long, slow journey (along the Mersey & Irwell Navigation, or the Bridgewater Canal) to the mills of

Manchester. By the end of the eighteenth century, Lancashire had become the home of cotton in Britain, Liverpool the main port of entry, and Manchester the main source of manufacture. It has been estimated that by the middle of the nineteenth century, Liverpool was handling in excess of 200,000 barrels of raw cotton per month, which was transported to the Lancashire mill towns. The arrival of the railway network in the mid nineteenth century boosted this trade even further.

Once at Manchester, the raw cotton was prepared: the seeds were removed, it was thoroughly washed and dried, and stored in the warehouses ready for dispatch to the appropriate mills. The cotton was spun or wove, bleached, dyed or printed. Printing had been pioneered by Haworth, Yates and Peel at Oswaldtwistle earlier, using blocks, though the process was greatly improved later with the use of engraved copper rollers. Initially all of these different processes were carried out in the one place, but as trade increased companies set up, each offering individual services, such as weavers, printers, bleachers etc.

When the textiles were completed, they were repackaged and transported back to Liverpool for export to many countries within the British Empire including, South Africa, Canada, Australia and New Zealand and India, as well as other countries such as China and Ireland. Trade also took place on the home market, selling to haberdashers throughout the country, and in cities such as London and Birmingham.

Following the change from water-power to steam power, mills opened in Manchester by the dozen. Mill owners were attracted to the town, and people were attracted here because of the work available in the mills. Manchester's early transport links, especially the canal network, which was superior to most, attracted a surge in warehouse building, and later new factories, all of which continued to grow. Soon the town was full of dark, grim factories, each with there own tall chimneys, all of them producing and adding to the thick black smoke that hung over the town's skyline; this was industrial Manchester. The centre became industrial, a mixture of warehouses, factories, mills, ironworks, foundries, timber yards, as far as the eye could see. By the 1840s, it is thought there were far in excess of one hundred mills in the middle of Manchester alone. One of the largest of the spinning mills was built by McConnel & Kennedy at Ancoats, alongside the Rochdale Canal.

*The centre of Manchester soon became industrial, with a mixture of warehouses, factories and mills on almost every street. This illustration depicts Portland Street in the heart of Manchester, with warehouses as far as the eye can see. That same street today is home to shops, theatres and trendy wine bars!* H E Tidmarsh

### Employment

By the middle of the nineteenth century, over 20,000 workers were employed in the cotton industry within Manchester alone, though unlike the other industries, the mills attracted a huge proportion of women, who worked mainly as weavers. Of course the mills employed men too, as spinners, but the mills also employed child labour. These were brought from the workhouses, and lived either amongst the looms on the mill floor, or if they were fortunate, in apprentices' houses. Young children provided an excellent and cheap work force for the mill owners, they were used for minor, laborious duties, basic labour such as moving the piles of cotton or clothes from place to place within the mill. But being so small they were useful, able to crawl under and between the looms, while they were still in operation to rectify little problems. The fact that this lead to a huge amount of accidents was perhaps of some minor concern, though greatly outweighed by the fact that as the looms were kept in operation it meant output was not affected. Eventually public and political pressure came to bear, leading to Government intervention.

The introduction of the *Factory Acts* began to improve matters by the turn of the nineteenth century, but the greatest step came in 1833, with the introduction of factory inspectors and far greater restrictions on the use of children in the workplace. In 1847, the passing of the *Ten Hours Act*, finally stopped women and children being expected to work both day and night, confining their time to a maximum of ten hours. Children were still employed in the mills even following this legislation, of course, though many were employed as 'half-timers' (what we might call part-timers today), they worked in the mills when not at school, this alternated between mornings one week and afternoons the other. However, this practice came to an end with the instigation of the 1918 *Education Act*, which made it mandatory for all under fourteens to attend school full time.

## Working Conditions

Working in the mills was hard, as conditions were created to the benefit of the cotton, not the workforce. The spinning mills were kept to a high temperature – normally around 85-90 degrees – with a high humidity factor created by steaming, to ensure the texture of the cotton. The men working here, were bare footed and stripped to the waist, even so, at times such as during the summer months the heat and humidity was unbearable. Comparing this to working in the

*In a seemingly short period of time the old town was full of dark, grim factories, each with their own tall chimneys, all of them producing and adding to the thick black smoke that hung over the town's sky line; this was industrial Manchester, a town filled with pollution, and an unhealthy place in which to live and work.* H E Tidmarsh

weaving sheds was like chalk and cheese; where the spinning mills were relatively quiet, the weaving sheds, with their looms were extremely noisy. So noisy, in fact, that the women here learned communication with one and other by lip-reading or sign language. Although the weaving sheds were humid, they were not as warm as the mills, so dress was different, clogs were worn for the floors were cobbles, and heavier, warmer clothing were the norm; even so, in winter the sheds were freezing and the weavers shivered nonetheless.

It was very unhealthy to work in the mills, apart from accidents (such as workers caught up in fast moving machinery or struck by loose shuttles that crossed the mill at high velocity), the atmosphere was hazardous: the humidity, combined with the dust and fluff off the cotton caused bad chests and respiratory problems. Mill fires were common, since by their very nature the mills were fire hazards: the wooden floors soaked up oil from the machines, and the fluff off the cotton could easily be ignited. Fires started from the gas lights being smashed, or from workers smoking in the stock rooms, away from the overlookers. Once a fire started it soon took hold and became uncontrollable; a huge five or six storey mill could be completely gutted in an hour or so. Only much later did the design of the mills change, steel framed mills were built, with concrete floors and built-in safety systems, these also had more windows which provided greater natural light.

## Different Lifestyles

With the mills attracting such a growing population, housing within Manchester became a problem. This lead to the building of sub-standard housing, back-to-back terraced, perhaps better described as slums. With an entrance at the front, along with a couple of windows, the house consisted of one-up, one-down, with no back door, windows or garden; with your neighbours property built on the back. These houses were built in courts, with one communal privy, which drained into a cesspool or pit, which was emptied only when full. Many of these places were made worse by shared lodgings, where entire families with several children lived in perhaps one or two rooms, two or three families to a house. These properties were generally located in the worst areas, alongside the rivers, where the poor air quality from the water, and the smoke and fumes of the nearby factories lead to illness. It was an awful existence, but the only one people could afford. Many of these properties were inhabited by the Irish population. Such was the poor standard of living that eventually a law was passed by the middle of the nineteenth century,

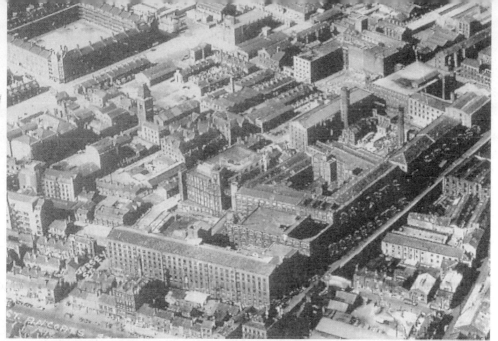

*Mills radiated from the centre of Manchester outwards into the suburbs. Ancoats, to the east of Manchester, was just one area that had more than its fair share of mills - including the McConnel & Kennedy mill, one of the largest of the spinning mills, alongside the Rochdale Canal. This aerial photograph shows Ancoats in the 1950s, and, although the industry was already in decline, the mills are still very evident.* The Author

banning their construction.

Living standards were such that it lead to disease: cholera struck the population on a number of occasions – in 1832, 1849-54 and 1866 – leading to many deaths, together with outbreaks of smallpox, typhoid and typhus. Many of these outbreaks were caused by poor water quality, much of the drinking water, especially in the poorer

*By the 1840s, it was thought there were far in excess of one hundred mills in the centre of Manchester alone. With the workforce consisting of men, women and children; entire families were often employed by the same boss.* H E Tidmarsh

areas, was extracted from the Irwell and Medlock; and the network of canals harboured disease through stagnant water. Their only respite was during the Wakes Weeks, when the mills closed for their annual holiday, and the workers all attended organised trips, on the canal boats or later the railway, to seaside destinations such as Southport, Blackpool and Morecambe, to take in the fresh air.

The slightly better off workers, such as the mill's overlookers – or tacklers, as they became known in Lancashire- lived in more conventional terraced houses, in long rows, where the houses were two up, two down, sometimes with individual outside toilets. Although they were still in sight and smell of the surrounding factories, the standard of living here was greatly improved.

The wealthy merchants chose to move far from the industrial population of Manchester, in the surrounding developing areas, in leafy Cheshire – places like Wilmslow and Sale were popular – or even as far afield as Parbold, where they built lavish halls, many of which still stand today. These locations were made possible, of course, with the advent of the railway network.

## Trade

Such was the trade that Manchester was now handling, that the first Cotton Exchange was built in 1729; however, increasing demand meant that within a relatively short space of time this building simply wasn't large enough to cope, so it was demolished in the late 1790s and replaced with a much larger structure in the early years of the new century. This process continued throughout the nineteenth century,

*The growth in the textile trade within Manchester can be measured, by the building of larger Exchanges. The first Cotton Exchange, built in 1729, was large enough to cope with the level of trade for much of that century.* H E Tidmarsh

*In the latter years of the century increasing demand meant that the Exchange simply wasn't large enough to cope, so it was demolished in the late 1790s and replaced with a much larger building in the early years of the new century. This process continued through the nineteenth century, leading to the creation of the Royal Exchange, a huge building, capable of handling all the business, commercial trade and export.* H E Tidmarsh/Author's collection

larger exchanges built to cope with increasing trade. This lead to the construction of the Royal Exchange, a huge building, capable of handling all the business, commercial trade and export.

Although Manchester was the centre of trade for cotton, and in the nineteenth century it was the largest trading area outside that of London, increasing prices for land and property meant it was no longer the ideal location for manufacturers. It became far more cost effective to relocate in surrounding mill towns of east Lancashire, such as Burnley, Bolton, Oldham and Rochdale. Transport had improved greatly with the competition between the canals and the railways, so

*The nineteenth century witnessed a huge growth in Manchester's population. With a vast amount of people coming here to find work in the mills, this inevitably lead to problems with a lack of housing. The answer was found in the construction of basic back-to-back terraced houses, built in courtyards with one communal privy. Here several families crowded into small rooms. A terrible situation that would continue through to the end of the century.* H E Tidmarsh

goods were being transported far cheaper than before; and more importantly, land prices, for mills and factories, and their continued expansion, was much lower away from Manchester. Instead Manchester became the trading centre, where merchants came to buy and sell, and the manufacture was carried out on the outskirts. As a result, Burnley, with its famous Weaver's Triangle, became the weaving capital of the world by the middle of the nineteenth century. At the same time, Manchester was regarded as a premier industrial city, yet it was only promoted to city status, officially, in 1853, by Queen Victoria.

**The Fall of King Cotton**
The cotton trade, although extremely successful and profitable was not without its slumps, the two most notable being during the Cotton Famine and the American Civil War, both of which hit the British market hard, and thousands of mill workers were laid off; yet, the upturn, once the crisis was over, was if anything, more dramatic than the downturn had been. The British cotton industry was capable of withstanding the ups and downs of the market, but a century later it was in serious decline. Low prices from foreign markets, where the laws regarding child labour were far different from ours, made British cotton too expensive, and witnessed the mass closure of the mills. Ironically though, it was the British who had taught the other countries of the world how to spin and weave in the first place.

# 5   RAILWAY MANIA

BY the early years of the nineteenth century, the transport of freight, between Liverpool and Manchester, had become the monopoly of the Bridgewater Canal, or the Mersey & Irwell Navigation, which had meant rates had risen significantly. Both Liverpool and Manchester merchants had complained about this, but without a credible alternative to rival the canals, their complaints simply fell on deaf ears.

A possible alternative to canals were tramways. Carts, pulled along wooden tramways by horses, had been used for many years by collieries, and now it was suggested that iron rails should be employed, thus making the lines more durable, as a credible means of transporting the freight between towns. Thomas Gray, from Nottingham, had pressed the idea with many prominent people, including the Prime Minister, Secretary of State for Transport, the Lord Mayor of London, but to no avail. However, a meeting between Gray and the Manchester merchants (arranged through his brother Charles, who was a close friend of Jeremiah Fielding, one of the more prominent of the Manchester merchants), received a much more favourable response.

Gray's suggestion of connecting Manchester to Liverpool by rail was warmly accepted, although it was not wholly new: the canal engineer, William Jessop, had first suggested joining the two places by rail, using horse-drawn wagons, in 1794. This was followed up by Benjamin Outram, who carried out a survey of such a line in 1798, however, his sudden death in 1805 brought the project to a close.

During the nineteenth century, England was an economic roller coaster: prosperity was followed by a crash, followed by further prosperity, followed by a lesser crash. It was a precarious time for investors, and not a time to invest in unproven schemes such as railways. Yet the demands of the merchants, lead by William James and Joseph Sandars, were to prove to be the necessary catalyst required to drive the idea forward.

James was something of an entrepreneur, who had invested in both land and collieries, and found the prospect of railways so interesting that he travelled the country, inspecting other similar projects. This travel took him to Northumbria in 1821, where he visited Killingworth Colliery and spoke with their resident engineer, George Stephenson,

*From their first meeting at the Killingworth Colliery in 1821, William James knew that he wanted George Stephenson to become the chief engineer on the Liverpool & Manchester Railway. Following great disappointment and turmoil, Stephenson would finally achieve that position, and, through his great foresight, would later be referred to as the 'Father of the Railways'.* Author's collection

who had just designed and built his first locomotive, called the Billy. The two men discussed in detail the possibility of a railway linking Liverpool and Manchester, and it was then that James pencilled in Stephenson as a possible engineer to construct it. Later that year, Stephenson would begin work on the construction of the Stockton & Darlington Railway, employed by Edward Pease, and from this gain even greater notoriety.

## Surveying the Line

The following year, William James, together with his two sons, William and George, and Stephenson's son, Robert, began the first survey of the Liverpool & Manchester line, wholly financed by Sandars. This was met with great hostility, from the locals they encountered, stone throwing was common, and the surveyors were attacked several times. It was a difficult time for all, and took months to complete. In the meantime, however, Sandars travelled widely drumming up support for the project. Provisional committees were formed in both Liverpool and Manchester.

James' original projections relating to the cost of construction estimated a figure of around £100,000; the respective committees called for the completion of his survey by the end of the summer, though delays meant that it was not finished until November. By this time, James was himself in trouble; he was being sued by his brother-in-law, which led to a jail sentence and ultimately to bankruptcy in 1823. The loss of James from the project meant that his survey was never collated.

In May of 1824, the respective committees of Liverpool and Manchester, instructed four of its more prominent members – Joseph Sandars, Lister Ellis, Henry Booth and John Kennedy, to visit various sites of railway activities. This tour included the Stockton & Darlington Railway, where Stephenson was consulted again, and Sandars asked him to carry out a survey of their proposed railway. Stephenson agreed, and arrived in Liverpool on 12 June 1824, and selected a team of surveyors, which included James' brother-in-law.

His proposed route was to leave Liverpool from the north, thus avoiding the gradient to the west of the town, and proceed through Fazakerley, Croxteth, Knowsley, through St Helens to connect with the collieries there, and carry on through Leigh and Eccles to a terminus at Salford. This survey was to face far more than just local hostility, it was to be opposed at every stage by the owners of the land that it intended to cross, and the canal proprietors, who saw this survey as the greatest threat yet to their monopoly. The canal owners had begun spreading rumours regarding the safety of the locomotives that would operate on the railway, claiming that they would cause fires, scare cattle, and make the use of horses redundant. But the greatest and most credible objections came from the Earls of Derby and Sefton, two of the most powerful men in the region, who objected to the proximity of the line to their respective estates just beyond Liverpool at Knowsley and Croxteth.

The survey was dogged with problems, with the landowners

obstructing the work by denying the surveyors access. This open hostility was most prominent on the estate of the Duke of Bridgewater, where Robert Haldene Bradshaw, head of the Bridgewater Canal Company, had instructed his gamekeepers to forcibly eject anyone found within the grounds. Eventually, through cunning, Stephenson did gain access to the estate, though it was far from satisfactory. In fact the entire survey would prove to be less than satisfactory: it was rushed, and on other parts of the proposed line, much of their work was carried out in the same manner, normally during the night by torchlight.

Despite these problems, the survey was completed by November 1824, and was made ready for inspection in February of the following year, but, by now, the projected cost of construction had risen to £400,000. The Bill had its first reading in the Commons, on 8 February 1825, gaining its second reading on 28 February. William Huskisson, MP for Liverpool, and President of the Board of Trade, made a passionate speech in favour of the Bill, and it was also supported by William Peel (brother of Sir Robert). However, it had its critics, and George Philips, a known supporter of the canals, spoke against the project. It was later decided, though without going to a vote, to put the matter before a parliamentary committee, headed by General Gascoyne, where the merits of the case could be studied in more detail.

The committee sat from 21 March, and called experts to support both sides of the argument. Francis Giles, an eminent canal engineer, was called by the opposition, to undermine the technical abilities of Stephenson. On 25 April, George Stephenson was called to give evidence; and he would continue to be questioned for another two days. All went well on the first day, Stephenson made some valid points regarding the need for an alternative form of transport to canals, however, perhaps because the first day had gone so well, Stephenson relaxed, and the next two days were to prove far more embarrassing. Here he was questioned on his survey in more detail, and was found to be wholly lacking. The opposition suggested that the survey was inadequate: it had clearly been rushed (doubtless due to the difficulties they had faced, but rushed all the same), and the calculations for the height of the bridges, embankments, viaducts, were so vague that the opposition were able to rubbish them easily. Stephenson himself was an easy target for the smart southern lawyers hired by the canal companies; an uneducated man with a broad north east accent who was inarticulate, they soon made him appear slow and backwards. The result was that the Bill was easily defeated. It was rejected by Parliament on 1 June, 1825, and as a result of its failure, Stephenson was dismissed from the project soon afterwards.

Regardless of this embarrassing defeat, the Liverpool & Manchester Railway Company knew they had to survey the line yet again, and approached John and George Rennie, sons of the famous canal builder, who were far more experienced than Stephenson at the procedure of passing a Bill through Parliament.

The Rennie brothers, in turn, appointed Charles Blacker Vignoles (an engineer in his own right) as their chief surveyor, who began his survey in July, and presented his initial findings to the committee in the August. It should be pointed out that Vignoles experienced far less resistance from the landowners and the canal companies than Stephenson; this was explained at the time as 'gentle persuasion' though it was rumoured later that the Rennies had bribed some of the more influential objectors – such as Bradshaw – by offering them shares in the company. Vignoles also successfully defused the objection from the two earls, by simply bringing the line further south and far enough away from both of their estates.

A new Bill was presented before Parliament in February 1826, where it passed through the House of Commons and was passed to the Lords in the April. During the committee stage, both the Rennie brothers, and Vignoles, conducted themselves well, and were vastly superior of that of Stephenson. It passed through the Lords, with only the Lords Derby and Sefton voting against it, and gained Royal Assent on the 5 May 1826.

**Construction of the Railway**
The Liverpool & Manchester Railway Company now had to choose a chief engineer to head the project. The Rennie brothers were the obvious choice, of course, but their overpowering attitude did not please the Committee, and they were reluctant to give them total control of the project. Therefore, in an effort to reduce the Rennie's overall influence, the committee suggested bringing in other engineers to share the construction. George Stephenson, despite his poor performance in Parliament in the original 1825 Bill, was still a firm favourite with both Sandars and Booth. Unfortunately, the mere suggestion that Stephenson would be connected with the project angered the Rennie's, who flatly refused to work with him (whether this was based on his earlier failure, personal rivalry, or simply a clash of personalities, is not known). The Rennies called for a meeting with the Committee in June, where they stated, quite clearly, that should they have to work alongside other engineers then they should be of a similar calibre to themselves, suggesting

alternatives such as Josiah Jessop, or Thomas Telford. They went on to state that, if Stephenson had to be connected with the project, then it had to be solely with the locomotive side, and not the construction. The Committee could not agree to these forceful requests, so ultimately, the Rennies withdrew from the project.

Later that month, the Committee contacted Jessop, who accepted the position as chief engineer, and Stephenson was retained as his assistant. However, from their first meeting, it was abundantly clear that the two men did not see eye-to-eye, and it was wondered as to how they could possibly work together on the line; this question was never answered, for Jessop died before construction could commence. Rather than begin the process of finding yet another chief engineer, the Committee decided to promote Stephenson (a position he had wanted all long), on 3 July 1826. He brought in Joseph Locke to be his assistant followed by John Dixon, William Allcard and Thomas Gooch. Charles Vignoles was still connected to the project, despite the Rennies departure; in fact, it is amazing that he was not considered as one of the candidates as chief engineer. Vignoles found Stephenson hard to deal with, and several arguments later, he resigned, in February 1827.

Work finally was put underway, though there was much to be done. Olive Mount Cutting was to be difficult, cutting through the natural sandstone; plus three tunnels were required to reach Liverpool, as the Common Council had strictly forbidden the railway to run across any of the town centre streets. Several embankments were also required throughout, to maintain the appropriate level, within acceptable limits. Fifty bridges, taking the line under or over the turnpike, and three viaducts, were required. And if that wasn't enough to contend with, the crossing of Chat Moss was a task in itself.

Much of the hard work, including the construction of the tunnels and cuttings, crossing Chat Moss, and the construction of the viaducts, all took place before 1828, and for a time, things looked bleak. Chat Moss, a notorious mere, although partly drained by John Gilbert in the previous century, was still a formidable place. Vignoles had begun the work here, up until his departure in February 1827, when John Dixon took over. More than 200 men were employed on this section alone, constructing huge drains, using ditches lined with barrels cut in half, in an effort to remove much of the surface water. Such was the difficulty of the terrain here that the men had to have boards strapped to their feet in order that they did not sink in the mud. After that, he began dumping tons of hard core on to the peat, in an attempt to build an embankment, but this was just swallowed up, without trace. Stephenson continued regardless, though his actions were mocked by his contemporaries, who could see little sense in dumping load after load of hard core with nothing to show for it. Even his workforce began to question his judgement. It has been said of Stephenson that if he had been an educated man, he too would have thought the process pointless, and quit; but he wasn't educated, just determined. Following three months of dumping hard core it began to hold; this was increased until it formed a stable platform on which to lay the track. On other sections, wicker mats were employed, several layers thick, which allowed the track to 'float' on top of the peat, in a revolutionary idea, but it also worked. In total, crossing Chat Moss was to cost in excess of £30,000.

Such was Parliament's distrust of Stephenson, that they commissioned Thomas Telford to review his actions and report back. Telford, ever a busy man, appointed his assistant James Mills in his place. His report was not in the least favourable, claiming that, in his opinion, progress was both slow and wholly disorganised. With this, many thought of having Stephenson replaced, even this late stage; though this did not happen, instead Robert Stephenson returned from work he was doing in South America to both assist and support his father. After this, things began to look a whole lot brighter and there was no further talk of replacing George Stephenson.

Further down the track, at Manchester, the original plan had been to create a terminus at Salford, however, a final extension through to Manchester (not authorised by Parliament until 1829), meant the construction of another viaduct over the River Irwell; this was supervised by John Dixon. With these obstacles overcome, the double track was laid, using fish-bellied type rails throughout on timber or in some cases, stone sleepers. Stephenson had used a gauge size of 4ft 8ins, which was the same size used on the Stockton & Darlington Railway, although this was not accepted by everyone as being the best size; other engineers, such as Brunel, used a much broader gauge. This came to a head in 1845, with the expansion of the railway throughout the country it was impractical to have different sized gauges; a Royal Commission was sent up in that same year, to investigate the best size; the *Gauge Act* of 1846 passed that all new rail should conform to the size of 4ft 8ins. Stephenson had been proved right once again.

Many celebrations were held with the final completion of the line, the first of these took place in Manchester on 15 September 1829, where many dignitaries were present, although the guest of honour was the Prime Minister, the Duke of Wellington.

*Although the* Rocket *is seen as George and Robert Stephenson's premier locomotive, this was not the first of its type: George Stephenson had designed the* Billy *in 1821, but the forerunner of the famous* Rocket *was the* Locomotion – *seen here in two very different pictures – that was used very successfully on the Stockton & Darlington Railway.* The Author

**Locomotive Trials**

With the line completed, attention now turned to the manner in which the wagons and carriages would be hauled along the line. Some felt that the use of a stationary engine should be employed to haul the carriages with the use of a cable, as used in some of the major collieries; while others looked to use the locomotives along the track itself, pulling the carriages along behind. There was some concern as to the reliability of the second suggestion: James Walker and Urpeth Rastrick, two eminent locomotive experts, were consulted. Finally, following exhaustive tests with stationary engines, it was decided that the best method was to use a moveable locomotive and trials of similar locomotive engines were organised at Rainhill, between 6-14 October 1829, in an effort to find the most suitable.

In total five locomotives took part in the trials, all of which were tested on speed, momentum, and reliability; they would after all, need to be capable of hauling carriages a distance of around seventy-five miles (the distance covered from Liverpool & Manchester, and back). The winner would receive the sum of £500.

The five contestants were: the *Rocket*, designed and built by George and Robert Stephenson; the *Sans Pareil*, by Timothy Hackworth; the *Novelty*, by John Braithwaite and John Ericsson, from London; the *Perseverence*, from Timothy Burstalls; and finally, the *Cyclopede*, from T S Brandreth. The latter two machines did little or nothing during the trials, more often than not, they were suffering from running difficulties. Similar results were recorded for the *Sans Pareil*, but Braithwaite and Ericsson faired much better with their *Novelty*, which might have won had it not suffered mechanical problems on the final day, making it appear unreliable. The clear and outright winner, though, was Stephenson's *Rocket*, which in all the different tests, had come out top.

**The Opening of the Liverpool & Manchester Railway**

The official opening of the Liverpool & Manchester Railway took place on 15 September 1830. A total of seven locomotives were used: George Stephenson drove the *Northumbria*, his son Robert handled the *Phoenix*, George's brother had the *North Star*, Thomas Gooch the *Dart*, and Joseph Locke had the *Rocket*; the *Arrow* and the *Meteor* were also in use. The carriages which followed were filled with dignitaries, the Prime Minister (the Duke of Wellington), Sir Robert Peel, William Huskisson, (Liverpool MP and President of the Board of Trade), Lord Wilton; and a twenty-year-old actress, by the name of Fanny Kemble.

The opening run is most remembered for the accident involving

William Huskisson. The journey had gone well until then. The party had departed Liverpool on time and had made good progress, stopping at Parkside, just beyond Newton-le-Willows, to take on water. At the start of their journey, all of the passengers had been handed a leaflet, explaining the route, and stating quite clearly not to leave the carriages during the course of the journey. Nevertheless, when the carriages stopped, some of the people got out to stretch their legs, including Huskinsson. Shortly after, an alarm was heard, heralding the *Rocket's* return, on the Liverpool-bound track. The crowd scattered, some hid beneath the embankment, others leaped into the nearest carriage, but Huskisson froze at the sight of the approaching locomotive. Unable to get out of the way, he was struck by the train, which broke his leg and severed an artery. He was carried back to the carriage on a makeshift stretcher, where Lord Wilton and his wife attended to him, tying a handkerchief around the wound in an attempt to reduce the bleeding. Vital time was lost during a disagreement that followed as to where was the best place to take the injured man to; in the end, it was decided that Eccles was the nearest place, so the *Rocket* was coupled to a single carriage and rushed at speed. He was taken to

*Two different pictures of Stephenson's* Rocket – *a locomotive that became famous for winning the Rainhill Trials of 1829, and infamous for causing the death of William Huskisson in the following year during the opening run along the newly completed Liverpool & Manchester Railway.* Author's collection

the vicarage there, where Dr Brandeth and a surgeon named Hensman attended to the wound; it was decided that amputation was the only option; although he died later that same evening.

The remainder of the party, reassembled in the carriages, and after re-coupling to the other locomotives, continued through to Manchester. In total over eight hundred people travelled on the trains that day, with a single death, that could have been avoided, had the passengers remained in their carriages as they had been instructed to do.

When the train reached Manchester's Liverpool Road Station, they were met by hundreds of people, most of them shouting abuse at the Duke of Wellington, regarding the harsh Corn Laws, others still vividly recalled the Peterloo Massacre, while many in Manchester wanted political reform and representation in Parliament, signified by the banners stating 'Vote by Ballot'; tricolours were also flown, and local weavers pelted the carriages with stones.

The official party were met by the 59th Regiment, though the ceremony was cut short, the Duke of Wellington made a short speech before being swiftly lead away from the hostile crowd. It was decided that due to the hostile reception and the incident at Parkside, that the party should begin its return journey back to Liverpool straight away. The first locomotives left at 4.30 p.m., while the rest left around an hour later. The return journey was not without its problems, it rained heavily on the way back (making things very uncomfortable for those travelling in the uncovered carriages) and many of the passengers had to disembark to enable the locomotives to climb the steep gradient at Rainhill. The main party reached Liverpool at around 10 p.m., though the Duke of Wellington had left the train at Childwall, to visit the Marquess of Salisbury at Childwall Hall. The Duke had also called at Eccles on the way home, to enquire to the condition of Huskisson.

Although the line was now completed and open to traffic, freight or passengers, there was only one station – Liverpool Road, in Manchester, which opened in 1829 (which was above ground, and the trains entered from underneath). The first station at the opposite end of the line, in Liverpool, was Crown Street, which opened soon after. This was reached via the tunnels cut through the natural sandstone, a steep gradient; so steep that the locomotives had to be hauled through by a cable attached to stationary engine – though on the return journey, the slope acted in their favour and the locomotives descended by gravity alone. Stephenson, Locke, Dixon and Allcard remained with the Liverpool & Manchester Railway Company, supervising maintenance and line improvements through to 1833.

*The railways formed a vital and integral part of Manchester's infrastructure, certainly throughout the nineteenth century and into the twentieth, not just in the track and the stations, but in the buildings created by the many different railway companies. Clearly one of the more notable of the buildings is the former goods warehouse of the Great Northern Railway which stands off Peter Street.* The Author

## The Dawn of Railway Mania

For Manchester, the railway not only brought improvements in transport, it brought industry and employment. Throughout the remaining years of the nineteenth century, the railway continued to expand, with much of it occurring in or around Manchester. It was clear that the creation of the Liverpool & Manchester line had inspired others in the region: the Bolton & Leigh Railway had started in 1825 as a tramway to reach the Leeds & Liverpool Canal, though within five years it had become a railway in its own right; the Bolton & Bury Line was opened in 1838 (though did not reach Bury until 1846) with Salford's first station, opening in the same year, with services not just to Bolton but also Wigan. The proprietors had received parliamentary approval in 1831, and their original intention had been to construct the railway along the line of the canal, by filling in the waterway, but following objections from the canals users, it was later decided to build the railway to run alongside the canal instead. In the same year, an idea concerning a possible railway between Manchester and Sheffield was on the drawing board, though was later abandoned due to the severe terrain. The idea was resurrected five years later, with a different route, and completed in 1841.

On a national scale, the railway network, though still in its infancy, was rapidly coming of age. Industrial Manchester felt the need to gain connections to trade in other parts of the country. Liverpool had been earmarked for a project to link it with Birmingham, under the title of the Grand Junction Railway, which received parliamentary approval in 1833, and was completed within four years. This was a significant move, for it also allowed connection to London via the London & Birmingham Railway. Manchester pressed for connection to this line and following many forceful meetings, achieved its aim with the introduction of the Manchester & Birmingham railway in 1837. Another ambitious project was the Manchester & Leeds Railway which had received parliamentary approval in the following year. Both of these vital rail links reached the centre of Manchester, at Store Street and Hunt's Bank, respectively, in 1844.

The success of the Leeds & Manchester line lead to another trans-Pennine railway being proposed in the following year. The Huddersfield Canal, which had opened in 1811, passed through the Standedge Tunnel, and the canal proprietors proposed to build a railway, with another tunnel, connecting Manchester, via Stalybridge, to Huddersfield. Within two years of work commencing the line was taken over by the LNWR, and opened in 1849 as a significant rival to the Leeds & Manchester line.

This age of railways was taking on major acquisitions. The Liverpool & Manchester Railway was taken over by the Grand Junction Railway on 8 August 1845, following an *Act of Parliament*. However, within the space of twelve months, the Grand Junction Railway combined with the Manchester & Birmingham Railway and the London & Birmingham Railway to be the London & North Western Railway (LNWR).

The changes in railway companies were in themselves causing changes to Manchester's stations. The extension of the Leeds & Manchester Railway at Hunt's Bank lead to the closure of the Oldham Road Station, which had opened just three years earlier, and the construction of a new larger station, called the Leeds and Manchester Station (though better known today as Victoria Station). At the same time, the Liverpool & Manchester line was redirected into this new station and the original Liverpool Road Station was closed. Later still, this station took on a higher priority when it was shared by the London & North Western Railway (LNWR) and the Lancashire & Yorkshire Railway; until LNWR decided to build yet another station next door, called the Exchange Station, which opened in 1884 and remained in use through to 1962. Today, the modern Victoria Station uses part of the old Exchange platforms. Liverpool Road Station, in the years after its closure was used as a goods yard through to 1975; since then it has become the Museum of Science & Industry.

The extension of the Leeds &
Manchester Railway in 1849, led to the
closure of the Oldham Street Station and
the creation of a much larger one,
originally known as the Leeds and
Manchester Station. At the same time,
the Liverpool, & Manchester Railway
was redirected to terminate here also. The
station changed its name to Victoria
Station following the Queen's Jubilee.
The illustration offers a glimpse of the
station in the Victorian era, while the two
modern photographs show the station as
it is today. H E Tidmarsh/The Author

Exchange Station was created in 1884, when the London & North Western Railway and the Lancashire & Yorkshire Railway, who were sharing platform space on Victoria Station, decided they needed a station of their own. This popular railway station, which stood alongside Victoria Station, remained in use through to 1962. And today, the modern Victoria Station still uses part of the old Exchange platforms. H E Tidmarsh

Manchester's third station was London Road, originally built in 1842, though the building was remodelled in 1862 by local architects, Mills & Murgatroyed. This was the home of two companies, the Manchester, Sheffield and Lincolnshire Railway (which became the Great Central Railway in 1897) and the London

London Road Station was originally built in 1842, but received extensive remodelling twenty years later by local architects, Mills & Murgatroyed. The station was operated jointly by the Manchester, Sheffield and Lincolnshire Railway and the London & North Western Railway. Each company operated its own separate platforms and booking offices. The station received further reconstruction in 1960, when it became Piccadilly Station. H E Tidmarsh

& North Western Railway. Each company operated its own separate platforms and booking offices (the LNWR on the right hand side of the station, the Great Central on the left). The building was remodelled again in 1960, changing its name to Piccadilly.

Manchester's fourth and final station (with the exception of smaller stations such as Oxford Road etc)was Manchester Central, built in 1872,designed by Sir John Fowler, with a huge glass arch in the style of London's St Pancras, and opened for the Cheshire Lines Railway. From 1 July 1880, the Midlands Railway (who had been operating in Manchester, from the London Road Station, since 1867) bought both Cheshire Lines and Central Station. They extended the station (by filling in the Manchester & Salford Junction Canal) and operated services through to Liverpool and Southport until 1969.

Throughout the remainder of the nineteenth century and much of the twentieth, Manchester would remain a major railway hub. They were used extensively throughout the war years, moving both munitions and troops. And, in 1948, they were nationalised. Investment in the 1950s, was followed by the now infamous Beeching Cuts of the 1960s, when several of Manchester's traditional lines were closed. Despite all of these changes, the city still maintained its high profile as a railway centre, and this was rewarded by the opening of new lines during the 1980s, including extensions at Hazel Grove and Windsor Bridge, along with the vital connection to the airport; and the complete transformation of Victoria Station during the 1990s.

*Central Station was built in 1872 and would be the last of the wholly new stations to open in Manchester. Designed by Sir John Fowler, it took its dramatic style, with a huge glass arch, from London's St Pancras Station. This was the home of the Cheshire Lines Railway. The station closed in 1969, and for a period it remained derelict, before being transformed into the Manchester G-Mex.* H E Tidmarsh

# 6 *P*OWER TO THE PEOPLE

THE Industrial Revolution had struck Manchester without warning or forethought, immediately transforming it from a mere village into an industrial town almost overnight. The consequence of this meant that throughout the eighteenth and nineteenth centuries, despite there being work in abundance, there would be mass poverty in Manchester. If things were ever to change, then the changes would have to come from the people, the working classes, and not the government, who seemingly cared little for their plight.

The suppression of the working classes had simply continued from the eighteenth century and into the nineteenth. Poor wages, together with high food prices, meant that many families were not just living on the bread line, but under it: starvation and malnutrition were common throughout the working classes. Poor harvests, recorded from 1810 through to 1812, further raised the price of corn, taking it to beyond the reach of the humble working classes. Matters were made all the worse by unscrupulous shopkeepers giving short measures, a common practice of the day. This lamentable situation eventually led to, one might say, its almost inevitable conclusion: civil unrest.

*Manchester's Royal Exchange, served as the very symbol of Manchester's commercial wealth. The poor working class starved as a result of the Corn Laws keeping the price of bread artificially high, the merchants and the money-men of the town continued to do their dealing within the grand enclosure of the Royal Exchange, seemingly oblivious to the hardship and suffering all around them.* Author's collection

**People Power**

The first of these occurred in 1808 when workers protested to their employers at the poor level of wages. What originated as a protest, soon turned to violence, and the military being called out to suppress the rioting mob. In the confusion, one of the protesters was shot and killed by the military. However, no matter how distressing this incident might have appeared, it paled into insignificance compared with the Exchange Riot of 1812, for this signalled that the suppressed working classes would no longer be allowed to continue.

A meeting had been scheduled at the Exchange in support of a troubled government, whose actions were mostly despised by the common man, though were endorsed by the Prince Regent who had taken over the duties of his father, King George III, as he entered the famous 'mad period'. Outside, a local mob, that had, understandably, been prevented from entering the meeting, had come along to protest. Regardless of their suspension from the meeting, some of the mob managed to find a way into the Exchange and started to disrupt the gathering. Shouting abuse soon turned to violence, and a riot followed, resulting in the military being called out to remove the protesters.

A few days later, and the apparently peaceful location of Shudehill market became the location for further unrest, when traders were accused by the people of massive overcharging on the sale of vegetables. Some of the people, deprived from buying their groceries by their inflated prices, began taking what they needed without payment. Once again the military were called to control the situation. Further rioting followed in June, and culminated in the arrest of thirty-eight weavers, who had gathered in Manchester to petition the government for greater parliamentary representation and reform. They were, however, later acquitted. Food riots ceased when the harvest of 1813 was returned in spectacular fashion. The abundance of food, now at lower, more affordable prices, made the people much more content.

There had been hardship experienced throughout the years of the Napoleonic Wars. However, even in 1815, when the wars were finally at an end, life although expected to be that much better for the soldiers returning home, in reality, had changed very little. The years following the wars were filled with demonstrations, working people protesting to a seemingly uncaring government that things had to get better. The greatest injustice, was the massive tax burden that had been created in order to recoup the cost of the wars. This, along with the distinct lack of self control, both at a local level and also a parliamentary one too, made the high level of taxation unbearable; these were the very conditions that had fuelled the American War of Independence and the words 'no taxation without representation' had returned to haunt the authorities. The people of Manchester, so resentful at the instigation of the unpopular Property Tax, petitioned parliament in the spring of 1816. The government did not 'get the message' and only angered the people further by imposing a tax on the importation of cheap corn, the Corn Laws thus depriving the working class of their daily bread. There was an outcry from the poor right across the nation.

The powers that be were now fearful of a full scale revolution, on the lines that had occurred in neighbouring France just a few years before. Their fears were seemingly justified, as in 1817, the Ardwick Plot, which involved the torching of Manchester as the prelude to a full-scale revolution, was uncovered and foiled. This grim discovery lead to the knee-jerk reaction of the forming of the Manchester Yeomanry Cavalry, to guard against any further treasonous acts.

## Political Reform

However, for all of those that wanted a revolution, there were many more that simply wanted political reform and greater representation. William Cobbett founded the Manchester Political Register, and held many meetings to protest at the lack of political representation. The first public rally for this cause, lead by John Knight, was held on St Peter's Field, on 4 November 1816. This was a resounding success, and led to the signing of a petition, with more than two thousand names upon it, calling for reform. A similar gathering was arranged for the end of the month, in order to review the success or failure of their petition.

As the political protests gathered more support, another rally was held in the same location on 10 March 1817, to once more, petition the government for change. However, the authorities had by now grown wise to these events and this time the gathering was broken up by the military. Undeterred, the protesters decided to take their cause, and indeed their petition direct to London in person and so began the long intended march to the nation's capital. Despite their firm intention, the march would not reach the capital – far from it, as the furthest they would go was on the outskirts of Derby – as the military pounced, arresting protesters en route. The arrests were nothing but a subterfuge to disrupt the march, for all of the Blanketteers were later released without charge.

The reality to the authorities was that in the new century things were already different. The forming of political groups, by what the authorities saw as radical reformers, that wanted to set a new agenda for working class reform. These reformers had appeared on the scene, expressing the opinion of the masses, that things had to change, quickly, and for the better. The item on the top of the reformers' agenda was parliamentary representation. The structure and distribution of the country's parliamentary seats had remained the same since Tudor times: in Lancashire – a county that had seen its population expand rapidly since it had wholeheartedly embraced the Industrial Revolution – and still returned just fourteen members of parliament. These opinions, contrary to the ideas expressed by the authorities, were generally stated in large, open-air meetings. Things were all the more prevalent in Manchester, who had been denied parliamentary representation since the Restoration.

Yet another meeting had been held at St Peter's Field on 8 January 1819, where Henry Hunt (1773-1835), one of the leading reformers, had addressed a crowd of around 8,000 people. Following the success of this meeting, other such meetings had been held in Stockport, Rochdale, Oldham, and many other places throughout the county. The reformers were a growing movement, that had gained the attention of the government and the authorities. Such was the reception in Manchester in January, that another, larger meeting was scheduled for August.

Although Hunt's campaign, for fairer political representation, was promoted by purely peaceful means, some within the reforming movement had much more radical ideas. Prior to the meeting planned for August, gatherings of like minded radicals had occurred on the moors above Manchester, where paramilitary style training and instruction had taken place, using pikes and even firearms. No political movement, no matter how well organised, is completely secret, and so the local magistrates were informed of these alarming developments. Hunt too had been told of the radicals' stance, and was equally alarmed that civilians were prepared to play at being soldiers. He made it crystal clear, in no uncertain terms, under no circumstances should anyone planning to attend the forthcoming meeting in August be carrying any sought of weapon.

The meeting was called for 9 August, at twelve noon, with the prime intention of discussing the reform of the House of Commons and the greater representation for the people of Manchester. However, the local magistrates – who had been asked to attend, to offer proof of the reformers good intentions – ruled the gathering illegal, and forced it to be abandoned. The reformers were undeterred, and made further requests to both the magistrates and the Special Constables, for the right to hold the meeting later in the month, on 16 August. Having received no reply to their requests they took this to be a begrudging sign of approval, and thus the meeting was scheduled to proceed.

## The Peterloo Massacre

St Peter's Field, standing close to St Peter's Church, in those times, was still just that, an open field, large enough for a gathering in excess of the 60,000 people the reformers hoped to attract to this meeting. On the day of the intended meeting crowds of people converged on the town, from around the region, each and every town and village had sent along their own party of people to represent their interests. As the crowds, which were thousands strong by now, neared Manchester they combined, forming a huge march, walking twelve abreast along the streets, and eventually along Deansgate to St Peter's Field. They all carried flags and political banners with such slogans as 'Fair Representation for All', 'Vote by Ballot', 'No Corn Laws' etc. Such was the expectation of the gathering, that the local shopkeepers feared rioting so closed and shuttered their stores early. By now the centre of the town was bustling with activity, yet the outskirts were empty, and a strange silence hung all around.

The magistrates, clearly fearful that if such a large and volatile meeting was allowed to proceed it would lead to further trouble, summoned the assistance of the troops: the Manchester and Salford Yeomanry lead by Captain Hugh Hornby Birley, the Cheshire Yeomanry lead by Major Thomas Joseph Trafford, the 31st Regiment of the 15th Hussars, commanded by Colonel Guy L'Estrange, were here to support, Jonathan Andrew, Constable of Manchester and the two hundred or so special constables. Command, between the overall forces, was split between the magistrates, lead by William Hulton, the local squire, who controlled the yeomanry and the constables, and Colonel Guy L'Estrange, of the 31st Regiment, who commanded around 1500 Hussars. Intense discussion had occurred prior to the gathering, where it had been decided that the magistrates had not the power to intervene to stop the meeting, and it was now impossible to halt it with a show of force. It was agreed, then, that the leaders, Henry Hunt, William Fitton, Joseph Johnson and Joseph Healey should be arrested.

*Three photographs depicting subtle changes in the appearance of St Peter's Square from the later nineteenth century through to the 1950s. However, in the early years of the nineteenth century this was still St Peter's Field, as it had been from medieval times – a large piece of open ground, where, on 16 August 1819, the infamous Peterloo Massacre took place.* Author's collection

On the morning of the meeting, at around 10 am, prior to the arrival of the crowds, 350 Hussars had marched through the centre of Manchester, with others mounted, and stationed themselves nearby, at Lower Moseley Street in a state of readiness – close by, in St John Street, were the Cheshire Yeomanry. The Manchester and Salford Yeomanry, being local and obviously knowing the ground better, had been stationed closer to the site of the gathering, in Pickford's Yard, and in the immediate streets off Deansgate, such as Byrom Street. In the centre of the field was a makeshift platform, made from planks which had been laid across the back of two stationary carts, from where the speakers were to address the crowd. The special constables were posted around the platform itself, in an attempt to be able to control the gathering crowd and arrest the leaders on their appearance. The magistrates had met at Mr Buxton's house in Mount Street, at around 11am, which overlooked St Peter's Field, and from which they could survey the meeting.

It has been estimated, that by the time the speakers arrived the crowd had swollen to around one hundred and fifty thousand people, many of them were women and children; all of which were unarmed, Hunt's plea's for a calm, respectable, violence-free

*People came from miles around to attend the open air meeting scheduled for 16 August. They combined as they reached the outskirts of the old town, forming a huge march, walking twelve abreast along Deansgate to St Peter's Field. They all carried flags and political banners with such slogans as 'Fair Representation for All', 'Vote by Ballot', 'No Corn Laws' etc. These two pictures offer two very different images of the lower part of Deansgate – one from the late nineteenth century with its trams, and the other from the early years of the twenty-first century, with its traffic congestion!* The Author

gathering had been adhered to. When the speakers approached the platform, including Hunt, distinctive as ever in his white hat (which he wore as a sign of Radicalism), the waiting crowd gave them a particularly warm and rapturous welcome. And the crowd surged forward, to hear the speeches, and contact was made with the special constables positioned around the platform, and minor scuffles – pushing, shoving etc – broke out.

Seeing these scuffles with the constables, and fearing that disorder was about to start, the magistrates gave the order for Deputy Constable Joseph Nadin to arrest Hunt and his other reformers immediately, without causing further disturbance. This was deemed too risky, and potentially unsafe, without the back-up of the military. The Manchester and Salford Yeomanry were summoned from their position nearby, and came in quickly along Mount Street, to assist in the arrest and the protection of the constables. However, the swell of the crowd around the Yeomanry caused them to separate, making them confused as to their situation, which was a little more than alarmed at the anger of this vast crowd. In some cases the crowd hurled stones at the Yeomanry. Although it has since been stated that in the panic the troops lashed out with their sabres, it has been proved, beyond reasonable doubt, that this was done not to injure the crowd, but to disperse them to allow them access to leave. No-one was hurt in this early scuffle, and only banners and flags were chopped down by the troop's flashing blades.

However, seeing this commotion, and thinking that both the special constables and the yeomanry were under attack from the hostile crowd, the magistrates summoned the 15th Hussars. As they passed along Mount Street, under the window of Buxton's house, Hulton shouted down to L'Estrange, that his men were under attack and that the Hussars should disperse the crowd at all costs. At the sound of a bugle, they charged into the tightly packed crowd, dispersing them within ten minutes, but at a severe cost: in total eleven were killed, either trampled by the horses or the panicking crowd, and it is estimated that a further five or six hundred people were injured, and taken to Manchester Infirmary. Today, the area of St Peter's Field is covered by the Free Trade Hall (originally built in 1840, but was rebuilt by Edward Walters in 1853), Peter Street and the Theatre Royal.

Later, Hunt and his companions were arrested. They were taken to Lancaster where they were originally tried for treason, and although these ridiculous charges were later reduced they all served prison sentences: Hunt received two and a half years, while the rest including Fitton, Healey and Johnson, each served twelve months

The incident was recorded in the national press as the 'Peterloo Massacre', in reference to the use of the Hussars, who the Duke of Wellington had gained victory with over Napoleon at Waterloo, just five years earlier. Following the tragedy, letters of sympathy and donations arrived from around the country, such was the feeling of outrage at what had occurred in Manchester that day. The matter was briefly debated in the House of Commons, though without an MP, Manchester could not voice its outrage. An enquiry was called for, but it never took place.

In the weeks and months following the massacre there were riots on the streets of Manchester, and in one serious incident a special constable was murdered. Equally, following the yeomanry being called to break up the rioting mobs, some of the rioters were shot and killed in the military's attempt to clear the streets. There was an alarming, almost unnerving tension in the air around the town, which the authorities felt as much as the common people; the authorities summoned reinforcements of further troops to Manchester, fearing that this was about to lead to open civil conflict. However, their fears proved to be alarmist and unwarranted, for nothing of the like occurred; slowly things relaxed, and returned to normal. Hunt and his companions were eventually freed from Lancaster Castle, returning to Manchester with a heroes welcome. Yet within a year or so, prosperity had returned to Manchester, which caused the reformers movement to lose local support and wane.

As for its great leader, Henry Hunt, he had attempted on two previous occasions to be elected as a Member of Parliament – once at Bristol in 1812, and again at Westminster in 1816 – and had failed miserably on both occasions. However, following the fame he had gained with his involvement in Peterloo, he stood as a candidate in Preston during the 1830 election and, despite being up against the Earl of Derby, the local candidate, Hunt was successfully elected to serve.

### The Fight Goes on
Despite the upsurge in prosperity experienced by Manchester, the reformers continued their campaign. If success was ever to be achieved, then it was going to take a long and hard fought battle. To aid the change, the reformers looked to gain the support of the press, in an attempt to win the hearts and minds of the majority.

The local press around this period had been largely ineffective in any political sense. Manchester's first newspaper, the *Manchester Weekly Journal*, had been founded in 1719, and had simply reported local events, though without any political bias. Things changed in 1821, when John Edward Taylor founded the *Manchester Guardian*, which proved to be an excellent campaigner for the reform movement, with many of its columnists being well-known radical reformers. At the time, the greatest campaigning was against the much hated Corn Laws introduced by the Conservative Government in 1815, that placed excessive duty on all imported corn, in order to make home grown corn competitive. Such was the harshness of these laws, that the poor people of Manchester were starving along with the rest of the country. Matters took a more aggressive turn when, in a desperate attempt to feed their families, following the severe harvest of 1828-29, they attacked shops and warehouses. Immense damage was caused and many of the people were arrested.

Calls for the repeal of the Corn Laws from outside parliament had simply fallen on deaf ears. To be effective, the campaigners needed to be on the inside. So, by the 1830s, the campaign, promoted by the people of Manchester, and supported by the *Manchester Guardian*, had reverted to calling more and more for great political change. By now public opinion and, more importantly, political opinion within parliament, was changing in their favour, culminating in the passing of the first *Reform Act*, in 1832. This led to the right, once more, for the inhabitants of Manchester to elect their own Members of Parliament, a privilege that had been denied them by Charles II in 1660. On 15 December of that year, Charles Thomson and Mark Phillips, Manchester's MP's were elected, and took up their rightful seats in the House of Commons.

**Local Government**
Three years later, Parliament passed the *Municipal Corporation Act*, which gave towns the right to seek incorporation; the right to elect their own town council and govern their own affairs. The people of Manchester desperately wanted that right, and a campaign was formed to achieve it. This was lead by two strong local reformers, John Edward Taylor, proprietor of the *Manchester Guardian*, and Richard Cobden, a leading reformer. Although many opposed such a right of self administration, the campaign was successful, and in 1838 the first Manchester Corporation was formed. Thomas Potter was elected as its first Mayor. This was followed by the *Borough Incorporation Act* of 1842, which gave Manchester greater powers locally; in 1846, the Corporation bought the Barony of Manchester from the Mosley family.

*The Free Trade Hall was erected on Peter Street by members of the Anti-Corn League in 1840, to commemorate the Peterloo Massacre. This grand building was later rebuilt to a design by Edward Walters in 1853. The building survives to the present day, and is currently undergoing massive alterations to become an hotel.* H E Tidmarsh

*From their tiny offices in the Newall Buildings on Market Street, they steered a campaign that would in 1846 rid the country of this intolerable legislation. Cobden and Bright's unselfish determination to help the working classes has been recognised by their statues in St Ann's Square and Albert Square, respectively.* H E Tidmarsh

*Richard Cobden and John Bright assisted in the formation of the Anti-Corn Law Association in 1838, which, within twelve months had changed its name to the Anti-Corn League.* H E Tidmarsh

Although Manchester now had parliamentary representation, the harsh Corn Laws had not gone away. To combat this injustice of the common people, the Anti-Corn Law Association, made up of like-minded campaigners, had been formed in 1838; it became the Anti-Corn League the following year with offices in London as well as Manchester. Its main members were: George Wilson, who became chairman, Richard Cobden and John Bright, who operated out of its Manchester offices in the Newall Buildings on Market Street.

They campaigned (through leaflets, which were distributed by hand or by the Penny Post from 1840, organised demonstrations, and its own newspaper, *The Anti-Corn Law Circular*) for open international trade, with the abolition of the Corn Laws, so that world markets could be formed, thus reducing the cost of corn and raising the standard of living. Although the *Reform Act* of 1832 had gone some way to changing the political position, it was still far from satisfactory. There was strong opposition to this movement, not least by the Government of the day, who described their claims as sheer propaganda.

Cobden, although born in Sussex, had spent much of his life in Lancashire. And, although his family came from a traditional farming

*Manchester's path to self-determination began following a campaign lead by Richard Cobden, which resulted in the town securing the right of incorporation in 1838. This effectively replaced the Police Commission and allowed Manchester men to stand for election to the newly created Town Council. However, although Manchester was regarded as one of the first 'industrial cities' in Britain, it was denied the privilege of becoming a city. This mountain was finally climbed in 1853 when, following another successful campaign, it was finally granted city status by both parliament and Queen Victoria – beating its neighbour and rival, Liverpool, by a massive twenty-seven years. The city's famous Town Hall, was designed and built by Alfred Waterhouse.* Author's collection

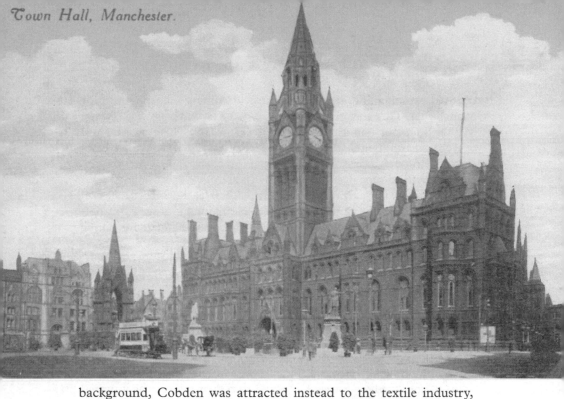

background, Cobden was attracted instead to the textile industry, setting up a mill in Sabden, a dark stone village that stands in east Lancashire under the shadow of Pendle Hill (today this former mill is used as the village institute). Here he produced cotton and dabbled in calico printing, before moving to Manchester in 1832. Cobden was a self-educated man, who had travelled widely throughout Europe and the USA. He was noted far and wide for his

talented campaigning, since his success at gaining incorporation for Manchester. This was put to good use in 1841 when he was elected MP for Stockport; once in the House of Commons, his powerful and persuasive arguments, directed at Sir Robert Peel (who had been elected Prime Minister in 1840), put increasing pressure on the Government to repeal the Corn Laws.

John Bright, a Quaker, was born in Rochdale, the son of a cotton mill owner, and one of seven children. He gained a basic education at a local Society of Friends school, and discovered a taste for public speaking; he was a natural, a man capable of holding an audience's attention on his every word. He, like his fellow reformer, Richard Cobden, had travelled in Europe, and was also elected to Parliament, as MP for Durham in 1843.

Following the Cotton Famine of 1845-46, which brought great hardship to the inhabitants of his native Lancashire, Sir Robert Peel yielded to public opinion and took the daring step of repealing the much hated Corn Laws in 1846. Although this pleased both the common man and the reformers greatly, it displeased the farmers, who feared a huge influx of corn from overseas, that would ruin their market ; as it turned out, this huge influx never occurred, and the farmers were safe, in fact, demand soured and the farmers benefited most from the repealing of the duty. Although Prime Minister Peel was a hero to the general public, politically his actions were suicide: the Whigs and Peelite Conservatives continued to support him; but the majority of the Conservative Party rebelled, and he was ousted as leader, in favour of Edward Stanley, the Earl of Derby; later Benjamin Disraeli took over the leadership. This change on the opinion of the government, primarily by the people of Manchester, lead to the sayings 'the Manchester School of Economics' and 'What Manchester does today, London does tomorrow'.

Following the passing of the *Reform Act* 1867, Manchester's MP's increased from two to three; the *Reform Act* of 1884 doubled this number to six. For many years the constituencies of Manchester returned Conservative MP's.

## City Status

Although Manchester was regarded as one of the first 'industrial cities' in Britain, it had been denied the privilege of becoming a city, doubtless due to its forthright political views. However, following a long campaign, it was finally granted city status, officially, in 1853, following a ruling by Queen Victoria. Despite the delays, Manchester had achieved its long-held goal of becoming the premiere city of the region – and beating its neighbour and rival, Liverpool, by a massive twenty-seven years.

# 7 $\mathcal{T}$HE MANCHESTER SHIP CANAL

THE economic success of Manchester's textile trade relied upon the Port of Liverpool to survive: this fed the cotton capital with raw materials, and exported its finished goods. For a great many years, the idea of creating a link to the sea for Manchester had been talked about. This was first approached in 1660, a plan proposed that the rivers Mersey and Irwell could be made navigable; although the plan was put before Parliament in the form of a Navigation Bill, it failed. Towards the end of the seventeenth century, Thomas Patten was using the Mersey to deliver goods to his Bank Quay copper works: although this had involved some minor navigation work, largely it was due to the tide passing up the river from Liverpool.

The first serious prospect at navigating the rivers through to Manchester came from a plan first put forward by the eminent engineer, Thomas Steers, in 1712 which used eight locks and weirs to create a workable waterway through to Manchester. Although the Bill was presented before Parliament, receiving Royal Assent in 1720, work on constructing the navigation did not commence until four years later; and it would be a further decade before goods could pass through to Manchester. This navigation, compared to others that Steers was involved in, such as the Douglas or Weaver Navigation's, was both poor in design and fraught with problems that were to plague it for many years: where later projects would use selective cuts to reduce or eliminate the natural meanders in the river, this navigation did not, this meant that boats had to negotiate the more winding parts of the river. The locks were small and unreliable, and, made from timber rather than stone, they needed constant maintenance; the waterway was prone to both silting and flooding making passage extremely dangerous. It had been the inadequacies of this navigation that had compelled Francis Egerton to construct his famous Bridgewater Canal; and with its final extension through to Runcorn in 1776, it became the first reliable link between Manchester and the sea.

The Duke's canal placed it in direct competiton with the Mersey & Irwell Navigation. The canal's superiority meant that the river navigation was soon losing trade, and the proprietors of the navigation offered it for sale to the Duke, for £10,000, though he rejected the offer. The navigation was later sold to a group of

Although the idea of making the rivers Mersey and Irwell navigable from Liverpool through to Manchester had first been mentioned as early as 1660, nothing more was done until the 1720s. The Mersey & Irwell Navigation was often unreliable, prompting the Duke of Bridgewater to extend his canal through to Runcorn in 1776. Tidmarsh's illustration of the Irwell offers a stark contrast to the modern photograph showing the same section of the river today. The picture on the opposite page shows the navigation of the River Mersey passing through Warrington at Bridgefoot. H E Tidmarsh/The Author

*Warrington Bridge and the River Mersey.* The Author

merchants from both Liverpool and Manchester, who invested heavily in the improvement of the waterway, rebuilding the weirs and locks in stone, and installing cuts to reduce the more awkward meanders. Where the Mersey & Irwell Navigation did have the upper hand over the Duke's canal was on the size of its locks, these were much larger, allowing much larger vessels than the conventional barges to pass through to Manchester.

Within eight years the arrival of the Liverpool-Manchester Railway brought increased competition, which ultimately lead to the decline in the Mersey & Irwell Navigation, which could no longer stay abreast of the race for traffic; the Bridgewater, on the other hand stood its ground well against its new rival – and later, compromise between the two rival forms of transport lead to a linking of freight prices.

Still the age-old dream of a sea link through to Manchester persisted. In 1838, Sir John Rennie proposed that the existing Mersey & Irwell Navigation could be made wider and deeper to create a ship canal, though apparently nothing came of the idea, for within two years a similar project was on the table, though this too was ignored. In 1844, the Bridgewater Canal Company bought out the rival Mersey & Irwell Navigation Company, later changing it name to the Bridgewater Navigation Company in 1872. At the same time, Edward Leader Williams, previously in charge of the Weaver Navigation, gained the position of General Manager and chief engineer and set about improving the performance of the canal by investing in a fleet of steam-powered tugs, which, quicker than the conventional barges, vastly improved delivery. The company was later bought by a group of directors from leading railway companies for £1 million, and the Mersey & Irwell Navigation ceased to be used.

Following the depression of the 1870s, the need for a sea link was all the more urgent. For although the Bridgewater Canal could handle small cargoes, the fact that the goods had originally passed from the Port of Liverpool meant that they were subject to duty; if a seagoing canal could be created it could effectively by-pass the port, and the duty. Many ideas followed: the construction of a ship canal, from the Dee estuary, along the Mersey through to Manchester was presented before parliament, but was rejected by both houses. In 1825, another such link was proposed, this time by the eminent engineer, William Chapman, called the Manchester and Dee Ship Canal; it would link Dawpool on the Wirral with Manchester; it was no more successful than the previous one, for although it was surveyed, it was never put before Parliament.

Matters took on a more organised role after the Manchester merchants chose Daniel Adamson, a local engineer and businessman, to take on the role of leader. The first meeting of all the like-minded individuals was held at Adamson's home on the 27 June 1882, at the meeting were many highly placed people, including the Mayor of Manchester; also at the meeting were two notable engineers, Edward Leader Williams and Hamilton Fulton. The conclusion of the gathering was that these two men should both carry out independent surveys of the prospect of constructing a ship canal, and report back their findings to the committee as soon as possible. Both men carried out their tasks, and returned reports for inspection by the end of the following month, though both men had completely different plans for the building of the sea link: Fulton had proposed a tidal canal, which was to follow the route of the existing old Mersey & Irwell Navigation, which would be extensively dredged to a depth capable of accepting seagoing vessels (this was on the lines of a project that Fulton had put to the merchants of Manchester in 1877, which had been turned down); while Williams, who was opposed to the idea of a tidal canal, recommended that a self-funding ship canal, using locks at appropriate sites was the only credible solution. The committee reviewed both the ideas put before them: the greatest problem with Fulton's plan was that Manchester was seventy feet above sea-level, so

*Throughout the 1870s thoughts of creating a ship canal between Liverpool and Manchester circulated from time to time but were never taken seriously. Matters took on a more organised role after Daniel Adamson, a local engineer and businessman, took control in the summer of 1882. He became the driving force behind the Manchester Ship Canal Project through to his resignation in February, 1887, and was replaced as chairman by Lord Egerton.*
Author's collection

Sir E Leader Williams                    Lord Egerton of Tatton

*Of the two plans put before the board - by the eminent engineers Edward Leader Williams and Hamilton Fulton - the Leader Williams plan was selected. Although the board experienced great difficulty getting its Bill through both Houses of Parliament, this was finally achieved : construction began in July 1885, with a grand ceremony at Eastham, where Lord Egerton cut the first sod, and Edward Leader Williams pleased onlookers by wheeling it away in a barrow.* Author's collection

the docks there, if fed by a tidal canal, would have to be sunk at a depth below the height of the road surface (Williams had estimated a figure of around one hundred feet). The committee came down in favour of Williams plan, using locks, though they felt that the section passing through the Mersey estuary could be feed by the tidal flow.

The Bill was presented before Parliament in November of that year, and it met with immediate opposition from the Port of Liverpool, which delayed it from being debated in both Houses until the following spring. Although the Bill passed through the House of Commons, it ran out of time in the Lords and so it was rejected. It returned to Parliament in the September of 1883, though further objections followed from Liverpool, not wanting to lose their monopoly as the North-West's leading port, and although this time it was passed in the House of Lords, strong objections from the Port of Liverpool, who claimed that the tidal canal through the Mersey estuary would cause silting that would increase the notorious Liverpool Bar (a sand bank just out to sea, which cannot be crossed at low tide) it failed to be passed by the Commons. To bring the merchants of Liverpool on side, the plans of the ship canal were changed dramatically; it was agreed not to use the tidal canal scheme, and not to touch the estuary at all: instead the canal would follow the shoreline of the Mersey (at first it was not sure as to which side the canal would take, though eventually the Cheshire side was chosen as the better of the two).

These changes swung the favour of Parliament behind the project, and the Bill received Royal Assent in 1885, though a proviso was that the new company would have to take over, by compulsory purchase, the Bridgewater Navigation Company so to eliminate any form of rivalry between the two waterways. It had cost almost half million pounds to put the Bill through Parliament, and it would cost the new company a further £1,700,000 to buy the Bridgewater Navigation Company, which raised the original budget – which had been estimated at around £5 Million – up by another £2 million. The problem facing the Manchester Ship Canal Company was how to raise the finances required, they would need £7 million before work could commence.

The passing of the Bill brought about rejoicing in the towns and villages along the planned route of the canal, the people realising that its construction would bring jobs and property: at Eccles, for instance, a big celebration meal was organised, Daniel Adamson was invited as the main guest of honour, on 31 August 1885, here a huge ox was roasted.

The raising of the necessary finances caused a split with Adamson and the rest of the board. Most of the directors proposed that the finances should be raised through London Merchant Banks, whereas Adamson much preferred the idea of raising the money locally by selling shares in small amounts to the people of the North West. Adamson resigned on 1 February, 1887, and was replaced as chairman by Lord Egerton.

The task of choosing a chief engineer caused great controversy. The board asked Thomas Andrew Walker, who was in his late sixties, and was currently employed as chief engineer on the Ribble Navigation project. Initially he declined the offer, stating that he was much too busy with his current project, but soon after, financial difficulties experienced by the Ribble Navigation Company caused work to be suspended and he was temporally released from his contact, enabling him to accept the offer made by the Manchester Ship Canal Company.

*The choice of chief engineer proved controversial. The board selected Thomas Andrew Walker, who was then chief engineer on the Ribble Navigation which had suffered financial difficulties and had been temporarily suspended. Walker proved to be a very competent engineer, and good progress was made on the construction until his untimely death in November 1889.* Author's collection

*Compared to the earlier industrial canals, the Ship Canal was to be cut in a more modern fashion. Although 17,000 Irish navvies were employed on the project, steam-powered excavators were used to handle the heavy work of cutting the canal the thirty-six miles from Eastham to Manchester.* H E Tidmarsh

## Construction of the Manchester Ship Canal

Construction began in July 1885, with a grand ceremony at Eastham, when Lord Egerton cut the first sod, and Edward Leader Williams pleased onlookers by wheeling it away in a barrow. Throughout the planned route – a distance of just over thirty-six miles – construction was divided into nine sections (although this was soon reduced to eight, when two of the smaller sections were joined together). With the work beginning at Eastham, and the canal cut towards Manchester, a large jetty was built to handle the delivery of the raw materials. Purchasing the necessary land to construct the canal was not without its problems, but overall it passed without too much delay. Construction of the Ship Canal, it being that much larger (and later) than the canals that had gone before it, was dramatically different: mechanical, steam-powered diggers and dredgers were employed throughout; although 17,000 Irish navvies were also employed, they were put to work in areas where the machines could not work, such as cutting through stone, rock and heavy boulder clay, then the traditional pick and shovel was used once more. Such was the size of the workforce employed on the construction that a special village was erected at Stanlow Point, near Ellesmere Port, to house them. A total of almost one hundred steam-powered excavators were used. Through the years of the work, literally hundreds of miles of railway track were laid, this was used not just to transport men and machinery, but to remove the spoil, much of which was used to make the embankments.

Apart from a huge engineering feat, the construction was a huge logistical one too, as the vast workforce had to be fed: caterers were employed to supply both food and drink to the workers at whatever areas they were working at. Temporary workshops were built at intervals along the length of the construction, these were used to repair and maintain the tools that were in almost constant use. Workers worked in shifts, day and night, working under artificial light to maintain the schedule.

All went well for the first two years of construction then Walker died on 25 November 1889, and after that things seemed to go wrong.

From that period onwards, it seemed as thought the project was plagued with problems: in the January of 1890, a severe winter froze the machinery, and brought work to complete stand still; when the frosts passed, flooding returned, making work difficult; this was followed by heavy prolonged rainfall through the spring months, which set the work back many, many months. And although some ground was recovered during the drier summer months, the following November flooding occurred again, this time far, far worse than before, which actually washed away a section of canal and some timber built bridges.

Problems such as these drove the costs up, taking it way beyond its original budgets. Further loans had to be arranged to secure the continuation of the project; although even these did not cover the mounting costs, eventually the Manchester Corporation was brought in, who took a majority seat on the Board of Directors, and made good the shortfall.

Construction of the Ship Canal involved difficult engineering: the planned route cut across fields, especially in the areas where the river meandered, and needed to be straightened out. Here cuts through fields were carried out long before the river was redirected, and the spoil was then used to fill in the old river bed. As the canal neared the Mersey estuary, a dam was constructed to hold back the water, while the building of an embankment, around ten miles in length, was carried out, using 13,000 piles, to separate the canal from the river.

The weir and locks once used on the Mersey & Irwell Navigation were demolished in March 1891, though for the time being, Brindley's Aqueduct was left in tact, so not to disrupt traffic on the

*One of the saddest consequences of the creation of the Manchester Ship Canal was the necessary destruction of Brindley's Barton Aqueduct: the structure was simply too low to allow the passage of shipping and had to go. It was replaced by the Barton Swing Aqueduct – a modern feat of engineering equal to that of the structure it replaced.* H E Tidmarsh

canal. To replace the famous aqueduct, Leader Williams had originally planned to incorporate the construction of two boat lifts (on the lines of the Anderton lift used to transport vessels between the Weaver Navigation and the Trent & Mersey Canal) though he later changed his mind to a moveable aqueduct; this is, in simple terms a huge metal tank, that's sealed at either end while it swings out, remaining full of water at all times. During the diversion of the Bridgewater Canal from Brindley's aqueduct to the new one, a short section of canal had to be constructed; though the first time this was filled with water the structure collapsed, and had to be replaced, thankfully the second attempt at filling was more successful. The swing-aqueduct opened in August 1893, and soon after work commenced on demolishing the original.

Leader Williams' plan included the construction of a series of locks along the canal to raise the level the necessary seventy feet. To reach Manchester this was a substantial engineering feat, for the

*By September 1891, a ten mile section of the Ship Canal, from Eastham Locks through to the Weaver Navigation was opened, allowing vessels to carry salt from the Cheshire Wiches. The Manchester Ship Canal was completed in the latter part of December 1893.* H E Tidmarsh

footing of the lock had to be dug deep into the canal bed, onto the natural sandstone, using bricks and stone, it was a massive undertaking; they were constructed from granite which had been transported from Penryn, Cornwall. In total, five sets of locks had to be built: Eastham, Latchford, Irlam, Barton and Mode Wheel; at Eastham, where the canal joins the Mersey, the locks are of three different sizes, the largest measures 600 by 80 feet, the middle lock 350 by 50 feet and the third was much smaller, to cater for barges – although this is no longer in use today.

Other problems were created with roads and railways having to cross over the Ship Canal. Where roads had previously travelled across the land being used for the canal, temporary timber bridges were erected; later some of these on the more minor routes were not replaced, as some of the lesser used roads were closed or redirected; in some cases ferries were installed to handle some crossings. The major roads over the canal were replaced by swing bridges, seven in total, which were fine for the amount of traffic they handled at the time; though today, the swing bridges still in use, especially around Warrington, cause delay to road traffic. During the road development of the 1960s, high level bridges were built over the Ship Canal, at locations such as Thelwall and Barton, to allow unrestricted crossing of the waterway.

But the greatest problems came with the railways crossing the canal: swing bridges were regarded as being highly unsafe, and creating tunnels to carry the railway under the canal was ruled out on the sheer expense. The answer was long embankments – on average two miles in length – seventy-five feet above the water. An example of this is the Latchford Viaduct, built in 1893. However, construction of these new viaducts set back the schedule of the canal by months, for not only did they need to be built, the railway companies insisted in excessive testing, using freight trains, before they would allow passenger trains across – in the meantime, the existing viaducts and bridges remained in use.

## Trafford Park

The Ship Canal's construction lead to the transformation of Trafford Park, from a country estate into an industrial park. This had been the home of the de Trafford family since Norman times and they had lived there, in relative peace and quiet, on their vast estate until 1761 and the arrival of the Bridgewater Canal. The family expressed strong objections to this waterway and their insistence that it could not cross any part of their land, lead to its route skirting around the southern boundary of the estate. Sir Humphrey de Trafford also objected to the arrival of the Ship Canal; though his death in 1886 lead to the succession of his son, Humphrey Francis de Trafford, who was less opposed to the arrival of industry, and agreed to sell a large section of his estate to the Ship Canal Company, which later became known as Trafford Wharf.

Later still, Sir Humphrey offered to sell his entire estate to the Manchester Corporation, who had thoughts of creating a public park there, though in the end the offer was rejected, and the estate was purchased by businessman and developer, E T Hooley in 1896, who started to create the industrial site that Trafford Park became famous for. Further development of the site occurred after the appointment of Marshall Stevens – who had previously been the General Manager of the Ship Canal Company – as the Trafford Park Estates manager. His job was to attract industry to the site, by promoting the excellent transportation of the Ship Canal. This was a huge success, attracting a great many businesses: Hedley Soap works, a subsidiary of Proctor & Gamble Alkali Company took a large site; a huge oil refinery was also built along side the canal. Trafford Hall, once the grand home of the de Traffords, survived for a few years after the family had sold the estate, used as a hotel, it sported a golf course and a boating lake – though later it was demolished to make way for more industry. Proctor & Gamble later relocated to the site, absorbing the Hedley works in the process.

*Although the directors and their families had travelled the length of the Ship Canal on New Year's day, 1894, by far the grandest ceremony occurred on 21 May, when Queen Victoria boarded the admiralty yacht Enchantress to see for herself, what many observers had already described as, 'the greatest feat of engineering in the Victorian era'.* H E Tidmarsh

## Completion, and a Grand Opening

By September 1891, a ten mile section of the Ship Canal, from Eastham Locks through to the Weaver Navigation was opened, allowing vessels to carry salt from the Cheshire Wiches. The Manchester Ship Canal was completed in the latter part of December 1893. On New Year's Day of 1894, a ceremony to mark the grand opening began with the first voyage along the entire length of the completed waterway, in total seventy-one ships took part, travelling from Eastham to the terminus, on board the lead ship were the directors of the company, their wives and family were in the second ship. On 21 May, Queen Victoria, who had travelled up from London by train, attended a ceremony and lunch at Manchester's Town Hall, before boarding the admiralty yacht *Enchantress* to travel along the Ship Canal to see, what many observers had described as, the greatest feat of engineering in the Victorian era.

## The Ship Canal in Operation

The opening of the sea link brought great trade to Manchester, ships from all over the world came along the Ship Canal, cargoes included: grain and timber, fruit, livestock, oil and coal. Goods were unloaded

Although the engineers had to overcome many obstacles in building the Ship Canal, one of the most tricky was allowing railways to cross over it. With swing bridges regarded as being unsafe, and tunnels too expensive, the answer was embankments - on average two miles in length - and viaducts standing seventy-five feet above the water. An example of this is the Latchford Viaduct, built in 1893. The exception was the Runcorn Viaduct which was already high enough to allow ships to pass underneath. H E Tidmarsh

on the dock side, and some where then loaded on to smaller barges for transportation on the conventional canal network – the Bridgewater Canal was connected to the Ship Canal via the Hulme Lock – to various destinations. In the early days, such was the level of trade that the company did not possess sufficient tugs to pilot the ships along the new canal, so extra tugs were leased from the Port of Liverpool. Co-operation between the Port of Liverpool and the Manchester Ship Canal lead to the general working practice, that meant that Port of Liverpool's tugs were responsible for ships entering and leaving the canal at the Mersey, whereas once on the canal, company tugs carried them through.

Blockages to the canal, caused by shipping were rare, although the company operated a strict policy whereby any vessel that did obstruct passage on the canal could be removed by any method the company saw fit. One of the major blockages occurred in September 1954, when the Norwegian timber boat *Borgfred* lost power to its steering while on route to Manchester without the aid of tugs, and blocked the canal; it took several hours work, using many tugs to finally haul it free. In March 1961, two boats collided causing one to sink to the bottom of the canal, which blocked the movement of larger vessels for weeks before the debris could be cleared. Silting was a constant occurrence, and the company had a small fleet of dredgers that operated all the time, removing sand that had been moved round in the wake of the larger ships, ensuring clear passage for those vessels with deep keels.

The Ship Canal has many docks, in fact, it is often said that the Port of Manchester operates along the entire length of the Ship Canal. Pomona Docks in Stretford were the original terminus, with further docks being added at Salford later. No 6 dock was the smallest, measuring just 850 feet, the largest was No 8 dock, which was 1350 feet long and 250 feet in width ( this was superseded by the new No 9 dock, built in 1905, and opened by King Edward VII, it measures 2700 feet in length). More docks were added to the complex in 1901, when the former racecourse site was bought. The first dry-dock on the canal was established near Mode Wheel in 1893.

The Manchester Ship Canal had delivered what had been asked of it: a direct and reliable link between Manchester and the sea. And, although it had surpassed its original budget – the final figure approaching £15 million – the level of trade that passed along the canal, through to Manchester, more than balanced out the cost of construction.

# 8 *T*WENTIETH CENTURY MANCHESTER

THE twentieth century was to bring massive changes to the city of Manchester. Some of these changes were for the better, in terms of housing and transport, whereas others, such as the death and destruction caused by the years of the Second World War, were not so welcome to the inhabitants.

## Political Changes

The 1906 general election brought many changes: nationally it witnessed the fall of the Conservatives and the creation of a Liberal government, though for Mancunnians, it saw the election of their first Labour MP. John Clynes, born in Oldham, the son of an Irish labourer, was successfully elected as parliamentary representative for the constituency of Manchester North-East, and would go on to serve in future Labour governments. The fall of the Conservatives was particularly distressing for Prime Minister, Arthur Balfour, who had served for many years as the MP for Manchester East.

The early years of the new century were filled, just like the latter years of the previous one, with calls for political reform. Some progress had already been made. The change to a secret ballot, achieved in 1872, for instance, had made eligible voters more relaxed at their choice of candidate. However, the case for women to gain the vote had been suppressed: the terms of the 1867 *Reform Act* stated that all 'householders were eligible to vote', but in those times all householders were men and definitely not women. The movement to gain the right to vote for women would play a significant part in the politics of the early part of the century, and Manchester would feature prominently in this.

Emmeline Goulden, born in 1858, was the eldest of five daughters of a Manchester cotton manufacturer. She came from a typically middle-class background, for after gaining her early education in Manchester, Emmeline was sent to a Paris finishing school, before returning to her native Manchester once more. It was here in Manchester that she met and later married a local barrister by the name of Richard Pankhurst. He later drafted the first Bill, placed before parliament by Jacob Bright (brother of John) in 1879 proposing the rights of women to have the vote; this Bill of course failed. Later that same year Richard and Emmeline married. This business took them to London, though they returned to their native Manchester in

HIPPODROME & OXFORD ROAD, MANCHESTER.

*A picture postcard featuring Oxford Road in 1902. Here the electric trams are a dominant feature of the Edwardian street. Who could have possibly thought that, by the end of the century, trams would have such a presence on Manchester's streets again. The photograph below shows the Metro-link trams at St Peter's Square.* Author's collection

Manchester's Midland Hotel *has been a landmark within the city for many years. This picture postcard dates from 1919. Compare it to the scene of 2002 in the accompanying photograph. The* Grand Hotel *still has a presence, even in its more modern surroundings.* Author's collection

1893, in the following year Emmeline was elected to serve on the Board of the Poor Law Guardians. Richard died three years later.

In 1900 she ran for the office of Manchester School Board and was successfully elected. Within three years their home in Nelson Street had been turned into the office and headquarters of the Women's Social & Political Union (WSPU), and she had been joined by her eldest daughter, Christabel, who had just gained a law degree at Manchester University. It was their dogged determination, and others inspired by their actions that eventually won the day.

The arrival of the Great War brought many changes to life in Manchester. The suffragette movement, although in contention with the actions of parliament, were patriots, and not only did they suspend their campaign for the duration of the war, they backed the fighting men wholeheartedly: the Manchester Regiment – which had formed in the latter years of the previous century, and had seen action in the Boer Wars – went off to war again, and would be present at the Somme and Gallipoli. The suffragettes solidarity with the government during their hour of need, did not go unnoticed by many of its MP's, and following the end of the conflict, minds had changed towards the idea of votes for women.

The greatest change to the voting system occurred in 1918, when the terms set in the 1867 *Reform Act*, that enabled all 'householders' to vote, were changed to simply 'all men over twenty-one had the vote, and all women over thirty'. Although there was no equality in the age of voting eligibility, the movement had won a significant victory, and a decade later the inequality between men and women's ages was made uniform.

Further changes were to occur on the political scene, with a gradual shift away from the Conservative party; for between 1918-1929 of the ten constituency MP's for Manchester, the majority returned were for the Conservative Party; in 1931 all ten were Conservatives in fact. After that victory, the gradual shift was to the Labour Party: by the landslide victory of 1945, nine of the ten were Labour. The changes to the constituencies in 1951 meant that Manchester changed from ten MP's to just nine, however, the political changes from Conservative to Labour continued regardless.

## A City at War

Manchester, along with its north west neighbour, Liverpool, became a prime target for the German Luftwaffe, receiving a number of incisive raids that would inflict massive damage on the city. In terms of destruction few buildings within the city remained untouched. And on a human scale, almost 600 people would lose their lives in

Deansgate, Manchester.

Deansgate dates from the Roman road that once followed this route out of the fort at Castlefield, though the thoroughfare itself gained more importance in the medieval period during the control of Baron Robert. These two pictures, depicting a similar view of Deansgate, the picture postcard from 1930 and the photograph from 2002, indicate the changes the road has witnessed in seventy odd years! Author's collection

*Manchester, like other cities, suffered at the hands of the Luftwaffe. The bombing reached its greatest intensity at Christmas 1940, later referred to as the Manchester Christmas Blitz, with major raids on the nights of the 22/23 December causing devastation to the city. In an effort to boost morale, the king and queen visited war-torn Manchester. This picture shows them visiting Stretford during 1941.* Author's collection

Manchester between 1940-45.

The first time the inhabitants heard the sirens, was on the evening of 20 June 1940. The people took to the shelters, not quite sure what to expect in this new theatre of modern warfare, though in actual fact they were in no danger, for it turned out to be a reconnaissance flight by the Luftwaffe. The first bombing raid came on 29 August 1940, and, although several bombs landed on the city, the overall damage was minor, and, most important of all, there were no casualties.

The intensity and regularity of the bombing increased throughout the autumn of 1940, reaching its greatest intensity at the Christmas of that year: two consecutive raids, on the nights of the 22 and 23 December – later referred to as the Manchester Christmas Blitz –

Throughout the years, Piccadilly has been an important and popular centre of the city. The following three pictures offer some insight of the changes that have occurred here through the years: the first photograph dates from the turn of the twentieth century; the second from the 1930s; and the last one is more recent – with the re-opening of the revamped and much loved Piccadilly Gardens in the summer of 2002. Author's collection

caused the most devastation to the city. The first raid began just after 6.30 pm and lasted until 11.30 pm. This was a deadly mix of blast bombs and incendiaries, dropped right across the city centre. Although the prime target was the city's warehouse district, many of Manchester's best known landmarks were hit, including Albert Square, the market place, Old Shambles, and parts of Deansgate.

By the following morning the damage inflicted by the raid was plain for all to see, as the blazing buildings stretched from Moseley Street to Portland Street. So severe was the blaze that the Manchester Fire Service had to call for reinforcements from other counties. Despite this assistance the fire was beyond control, and the Royal Engineers had to demolish several buildings.

Later that evening, at around 7 pm the second raid began. This time activity was concentrated around Piccadilly. Once again incendiary devices were used to great effect, causing a blazing inferno that was still well alight the following morning. The severity of the fire, fed by a north-east wind, gave concern that it might spread and engulf the entire city the city, and lead to the stark decision to demolish several buildings, many of them unaffected by the bombing, in an attempt to create a fire break. Victims during this second raid included the Free Trade Hall, Manchester's symbol of freedom. Other sites affected included the Cathedral, and Exchange and Victoria Station. The fatalities of the combined raids passed three hundred and fifty, and a further five hundred people were seriously injured. Thankfully, the city's children had been evacuated to the safety of the surrounding countryside.

The third of the heaviest bombing raids on Manchester came on the evening of 1 June 1941. Although this was one of the shortest raids, lasting just over an hour, the destruction was no less severe. This time the bombing was concentrated to the west of Manchester, causing damage to property in Derby Street and Southall Street, as well as Assize Court, and the Manchester College of Technology.

The war was hard on the civilian population of cities such as Manchester, and so it was understandable that thousands packed Manchester's Streets on 8 June, to celebrate V E Day. The celebrations began officially at 11.30 am outside the Cathedral, followed by the official announcement by the Lord Mayor on the Town Hall steps later that afternoon.

**Housing**

Manchester, as an urban environment, had been expanding since the Industrial Revolution, and the population had mirrored this trend:

*The city's famous cathedral, dating from medieval times, is still a dominant feature in twenty-first century Manchester. Although steeped in history, the building does not seem at all out of place now surrounded by more modern structures.* The Author

by the 1920s, Manchester's population had surpassed 730,000. Unfortunately, at the start of the twentieth century, Manchester was still filled with the slums of the previous century, and in no fit state to cope with this population boom. Although these homes ought to have been condemned and demolished, the ever expanding population was causing massive overcrowding, and had led to many properties remaining in use. Nevertheless, the need to improve housing was of dire need. Manchester City Council took its first steps to alleviate this problem in 1904, with the building of basic flats in the more needy parts of the city. However, the greatest change in housing came with the construction of the Burnage Garden Village –

*Manchester and its inhabitants suffered throughout the two world wars. Many young Manchester men went off to fight in the Great War and failed to return. The Cenotaph was built in St Peter's Square to remember them. When this picture of the Cenotaph was taken in 1923, few could have possibly imagined that another world war was just around the corner and once again, many Manchester men would fail to return.* Author's collection

a development comprising over one hundred modern houses, with gardens, hot and cold running water, and electric lighting – on the outskirts of the city centre in 1907. This early success was followed up in 1911, with another three hundred semi-detached houses built at Chorlton-cum-Hardy.

The city centre was still filled with slum housing, however, and it would take until 1930 before things began to move in the right direction. The passing of the 1930 *Slum Clearance Act,* enabled Manchester City Council to compulsory purchase the worst of the slums and demolish them. And the *Manchester Extension Act,* passed later the same year, allowed the City Council to extend the city boundaries, to include Wythenshawe. It was here at Wythenshawe that the council had its most ambitious plan – to create a new housing estate, large enough to accommodate 100,000 residents. The land was donated by Sir Ernest and Lady Simon, and the new estate was designed by Barry Parker. Work began in earnest and by the end of the decade over eight thousand houses had been built. Unfortunately building work was suspended with the arrival of the Second World War, though was resumed in 1945.

Following the devastation left by the war years, the need for further housing to cope with the ever-expanding population of Manchester was more urgent than before the war. Leonard Cox, Lord Mayor of Manchester, promised the inhabitants of Manchester that a 'fairer city' would be created in the wake of the devastation. The man given the responsibility of achieving this goal was the city surveyor, Robert Nicholas. His vision, clearly laid out in the 1945 Plan, saw a Manchester completely reborn; gone would be the old Victorian city, and in its place would be a modern, hi-tech, city fit for the citizens of the second half of the twentieth century and beyond. His idea was to create new housing estates, like satellites around the outside of the city, in locations such as Irlam, Sale, Partington and

*This picture postcard offers five popular scenes of Manchester during the 1950s: the Old Shambles, the Grand Hotel, St Peter's Square, St Ann's Square – looking remarkably different to present day prior to it becoming a pedestrian area, and Piccadilly gardens.* Author's collection

*Following the duration of the Second World War the football league resumed in 1946. In this picture taken in that year, the newly signed manager of Manchester United, Matt Busby, meets his team. Together they would become an award-winning side. Today, of course, Manchester United is by far the wealthiest club in the Premiere League.* Author's collection

Middleton. The first of these new residential areas was created at Hulme, located to the south of the city centre, with the Bentley Council Housing Estate.

However, despite many of the great plans that had been put forward, in the immediate years following the Second World War, the shortage of housing, combined with the shortage of materials, led to the continued construction of prefab housing begun during the war years, designed to tide people over the temporary crisis. And, although some of the proposals made in the original 1945 Plan were enacted upon, many had been dismissed by Manchester City Council as being too progressive or simply too expensive.

The next great change to Manchester came in the long awaited 1961 Redevelopment Plan, which was directed at improving the quality of life of the citizens of Manchester, and addressed their concerns in a number of areas, including housing, shops, education, recreation, industry, city centre development, minerals, transport, communications, environmental issues, public services, culture and health.

New legislation awarded to councils in the area of compulsory purchase orders, gave the 1961 Plan teeth, when it came to the tricky subject of housing. Even by the 1960s, there were still a great many examples of poor housing within the city's boundaries that urgently needed addressing, and this plan clearly demonstrated a decade of investment, which would involve both the demolition and generation of new, modern housing. It was an ambitious plan, with a total figure of more than 35,000 new homes planned for construction (over 20,000 of which were earmarked to be built within the city centre alone) but it went much further than housing concerns, as it also addressed the building of new schools within the outer areas of the city.

The focus of regeneration was also on the outer districts of the new city. This plan finally saw the implementation of Nicholas's satellite districts, with massive housing estates created in areas such as Hulme, Hyde, Langley and Hattersley. However, the housing shortage of the 1960s, lead to the authorities adopting modern methods of quick, easy to build, housing units; the result was flats, some high-rise, others two and three storey maisonettes. At Hulme, the emphasis was on quantity not quality and what was created were concrete jungles. Known as the Crescents, they consisted of four very distinctive curved blocks of flats, which were both poorly designed and poorly built, and meant that within a short space of time they were decaying, and soon became a nightmare for those that lived there.

The first of Manchester's high-rise flats were built here at Langley. Standing thirteen storeys high, the three tower blocks dominated the skyline. These new districts became overspill areas for the city centre. However, the downside of this redevelopment was the demolition of the terraced houses that had previously stood in their place; they might have been poor, but within these areas there was a community spirit, a spirit that had got the residents through the worse times of the Second World War. Now re-housed in these apartments in the sky, the community spirit was gone. Inner-city housing was becoming the buzz-word of the age. Where previous plans had suggested that housing should be spread throughout the surrounding districts – in fact new districts had been created to achieve this aim – this new thinking was that inner city living was to be the new ideal; living in the city centre meant that travelling to work would soon be a thing of the past! This was later acted upon: Wimpey Homes constructed a new estate, consisting of almost 200 new houses, between Deansgate and the Granada Studios in 1979.

Despite the best intentions of the city planners, the 'modern estates' erected in the 1960s and 1970s would, within a decade, become the poor housing of the latter twentieth century, and soon became as notorious as the Victorian slums of the nineteenth century. The concrete jungles became a place of insecurity and neglect. The concrete structures crumbled, and the residents forced to live in these substandard environments suffered.

Much talk was made during the 1980s about the unsatisfactory situation for the residents living in these slums and new homes had to be built. But despite all the talk, the residents of estates, such as those in Hulme, continued to suffer, until 1992, when Manchester applied for and won the backing of the government's City Challenge scheme of regeneration. Over £35 million of central government money was pumped into the area, and a new partnership called the Hulme Regeneration Limited, by Manchester City Council and the construction company AMEC set about transforming the area. The Crescents were demolished, to the cheers of the residents, and 3,000 new modern homes were built to replace them. Other housing estates, such as those seen around Miles Platting and Ancoats, which had been built in the 1950s and were showing their age, were both modernised and rejuvenated as part of the Single Regeneration Budget.

Another problem area, named Fort Ardwick, a series of high-rise flats built in the early 1960s, were condemned as being unfit for human habitation and were demolished in the 1990s, and the 600 families that had lived there were given modern terraced housing, which was a much more attractive place to live.

## A Modern Transport Policy

The ambitious 1961 Plan, not only looked at housing, but also addressed the issue of ring roads, first mentioned in the 1945 Plan. Once again, a total of three ring roads were scheduled: an inner, an intermediate and an outer. However, despite the planners' best intentions, none of these planned highways were acted upon, for in the following year, the SELNEC (South East Lancashire and North East Cheshire) Highway plan was published, with the recommendation of the construction of two new roads – the Northenden Bypass and the Sharston Bypass – to relieve congestion in and around the city. In later years, both of these roads would be linked and would eventually form the much heralded Outer Ring Road. Another new road, the Mancunian Way, a high level dual carriageway, was constructed in 1966 to link East Manchester with Trafford Park, and became the country's very first urban motorway.

Plans to improve public transport in and around the city had been originally set in motion by the forming of the SELNEC Passenger Transport Authority in 1968. One of their first proposals had been the construction of the Picc-Vic Tunnel, to link the city's two main railway station underground. However, despite work commencing on this ambitious plan, the project was later abandoned.

The next significant change in transport came in the 1980s, in the form of a modern tram system, known as the Metrolink, designed to connect Manchester ideally with all of its outlying districts. It was both a radical and ambitious move, though one that was in line with modern thinking that looked to reduce car use in the inner city, and enhance the use of public transport instead. A demonstration of the proposed modern trams was put on display in Manchester in the summer of 1987. However, despite the terrific reception the demonstration had received, construction of the Metrolink would not commence until 1991.

The Metrolink first came to life with the conversion of the old Bury and Altrincham railways lines into tramways, and the further laying of tram lines on the city's main streets. Therefore, the first Metrolink route was one that linked Bury, Manchester and Altrincham, though the sections were opened individually: Manchester to Bury opened first, on 6 April 1992, followed by the Altrincham route on 15 June, and finally connection between Victoria and Piccadilly Stations opening on 20 July. The service has proved, despite its critics, to be an overwhelming success. Its success lead to plans for its continued expansion: lines linking Salford Quays; Eccles, Manchester Airport; Wythenshawe; Oldham and Rochdale; and even Ashton-under-Lyme continue.

## The Story of Manchester Airport

Manchester's first commercial airfield had opened at Wythenshawe in 1928, with scheduled flights to the coastal resorts of Blackpool and Southport. However, within the space of just two years, the demand for flights led to Manchester City Council offering the use of land at Barton, on the outskirts of Eccles to construct a larger, more permanent airport. However, although the facilities at Barton were vastly superior to those at Wythenshawe, it was clear at an early stage that this airfield also had a limited life span, and within a few short years calls were being made for a much larger facility to be created to cope with the ever-increasing demand for air traffic. A new site was found, this time to the south of the city at Ringway, and work commenced on construction in 1935, and the new airport was open for its first passengers within three years. The thirst for air-travel was slower throughout the decade than had originally been expected, and the four grass runways remained in use through to the start of the Second World War, when concrete runways replaced them. They would be replaced again after the war, this time with smoother tarmac runways.

The airport had seen pre-war passenger numbers of around 8,000 per annum, leap to well in excess of 10,000 per year after the war; this upward trend would continue, as by the 1950s the airport was handling more than 150,000 passengers each year. New terminals were constructed at the airport from the late 1950s through to the early 1960s. Prince Philip, Duke of Edinburgh opened the new terminal in 1962. By the end of the decade, passenger numbers had surpassed one million per annum and would continue to rise throughout the following decade.

Plans to expand the size and service of the airport were laid out in a plan of 1984. The airport changed ownership two years later, when the Manchester Airport PLC was formed, with the shareholders consisting of the ten districts of the Greater Manchester Metropolitan Council. The new plans recommended that should the airport wish to remain the north-west largest, it would have to undergo much more expansion and modernisation. Their prime proposal was the construction of a second terminal. These plans were readily accepted and the new terminal, with its vital rail link, was opened in March 1993, to cater for the airport's annual turnover of around twelve million passengers.

With this completed, plans were submitted for the construction of a second runway. This proposal sparked massive protest, both from residents that would be affected by the new runway, and from eco-warriors, protesting at the wholesale carving up of the countryside. Nevertheless, despite massive objections, and civil unrest, the construction of the second runway commenced.

## City Centre Development

The development of Manchester City Centre was something that had to be addressed following the excessive damage caused to the city centre by the wartime bombing. For the first time in its history, the future of Manchester could be decided in one plan, which afforded the planners the opportunity to design a new modern city. It is fair to say that for the time, they had in mind quite radical ideas of making the centre open, with spacious gardens, Parisian styled tree-lined boulevards and precincts between the buildings. However, as idealistic as this plan undoubtedly was, and in many ways it was clearly ahead of its time, the cost of such a massive redevelopment, immediately after the long war years and with the country still in massive debt, made much of the plan prohibitive.

The next time that such matters were raised was during the writing of the 1961 Plan. However, although this dealt with the restructuring of the city centre, it was later excluded when being ratified by the Ministry of Housing & Local Government. Manchester City Council began work on reconstructing a new document that was to cover the redevelopment of the city centre, which was eventually published as the 1967 City Development Plan. Although supposedly a new plan, the contents of the new proposals mirrored in broad terms the original proposals of the 1945 Nicholas plan; there was no mention, for instance, of incorporating any of the surviving Victorian architecture in the new city. The prime consideration throughout the 1967 document was with transport, inner-city housing, and the shopping complex.

The city centre was deemed a Comprehensive Development Area, and the planners now wanted to transform Manchester's rundown shops into the cutting edge of modern shopping experience. The result was the Arndale Centre, designed by Wilson & Womersley, as a modern, self-contained shopping centre, completely enclosed, offering market stalls and modern shops in arcades, where shoppers would be away from the elements of the British weather. The complex was to be far more than just an indoor market, however, for above it combined both office space and residential accommodation too. The project was slow to develop, however, and would take almost twenty years to complete; although at its completion in the early 1980s, it was the largest indoor shopping area in the whole of Europe. However, almost from day one, the centre received bad press and was the butt of many poor jokes.

The city centre pioneered the way for pedestrian only areas: both St Ann's Square and King Street were the first of several areas to be

*The Arndale Centre came about through the creation of the Comprehensive Development Area. The idea was to create a modern shopping experience, and the centre was designed by architects Wilson & Womersley, as self-contained shopping centre, completely enclosed, offering market stalls and modern shops in arcades, where shoppers would be away from the elements of the British weather. However, the project was slow to develop, taking almost twenty years to complete, and from day one, the centre received bad press and was the butt of many poor jokes. This photograph shows the centre from Market Street.* The Author

Manchester became a victim of the long-time troubles of Northern Ireland on Saturday, 15 June 1996, when the IRA exploded a huge device on Corporation Street. The explosion caused massive devastation, effectively ripping the heart out of the city centre. Through hard work, and major reinvestment, the centre of the city has not only be restored, but beautifully transformed. These three photographs show Corporation Street, the Exchange, and the newly created Exchange Square on the eve of the Commonwealth Games held in the city in July 2002. The Author

cordoned off from traffic. In an attempt to improve matters, the City Centre Local plan was produced in 1984, which would guide the alterations to the centre of Manchester through to the close of the century, with all work being undertaken by the newly created Central Manchester Development Corporation.

One area of the city centre that had gone unnoticed, was that of Castlefield and land alongside the railway, with its continued decline being made all the worse with the closure of Central Station in 1966, and the later closure of the nearby Liverpool Road Goods Depot. Matters were discussed by the GMC, and by 1978 the land around Castlefield, including the old goods yards, were purchased, and designated as an area of conservation. Work soon began excavating the old Roman fort, and the Urban Heritage Park opened there in 1982. Throughout the next couple of years, further work was carried out, including the creation of the Museum of Science and Industry, the Air and Space Gallery. Much needed revenue from tourism was attracted with the transformation of the old Grape Street Warehouse into the Granada Studio Tours, at a cost approaching £8 Million, and the regeneration of the canals that converge at Castlefield. Today Castlefield, with its wealth of local history from the Roman occupation and throughout the Industrial Revolution, is one of the most popular tourist attractions in the region.

Whereas the Arndale Centre, in city centre Manchester, had come to epitomise everything that had been wrong about the town planning and building phases of the 1960s and indeed 1970s, the Trafford Centre, created in the 1990s, has proved to be the success it was claimed to be and perhaps points the way to out of town shopping in the future. With over 8,000 employees working within this centre, ideally situated for road links with the post industrial backdrop of the Manchester Ship Canal, the Trafford Centre is by far the largest shopping complex in the North-West region.

The most significant change to the appearance of the city centre came without warning, and occurred on Saturday, 15 June 1996, when the IRA exploded a huge device. The explosion caused massive devastation, and in the following years the centre of Manchester's shopping district was completely reformed, with the new Marks & Spencer store as its centrepiece.

**Local Government Changes**
Manchester's Lancashire heritage changed in the 1970s. The passing of the *Local Government Act* of 1972, lead to the creation of six new metropolitan county councils: in the north-west this meant the

forming of two new counties: Merseyside and SELNEC (South East Lancashire and North East Cheshire – later known as Greater Manchester). This new county would witness combining of ten district councils: Manchester, Bolton, Wigan, Rochdale, Salford, Bury, Trafford, Oldham, Stockport and Tameside. The new members of the Greater Manchester County Council were elected on 12 April 1973, and would form the GMC on 1 April 1974.

These new county councils, created primarily by the Labour Government, had a short life span however, for they were abolished by the Conservatives in 1986, and replaced by the forming of unitary authorities made up of their constituent boroughs. Within Greater Manchester, Altrincham and Sale, both previously in Cheshire, combined to create Trafford; whilst Ashton-under-Lyne, together with its smaller neighbours, Stalybridge, Hyde and Mossley, became Tameside.

## Olympic Challenge

Manchester made a play for greater world recognition in 1990, with its bid to host the 1996 Olympic Games, only to see it awarded to Atlanta instead. Undeterred, they launched another bid in 1992, this time for the 2000 Olympic Games. Both of these bids would have a number of influential spin-offs that would benefit Manchester in the long run.

The bid for the 1996 Olympics was geared mainly by the private sector, and headed by a group of Manchester businessmen. The centre of the proposed facilities were to be at Dumplington on the outskirts of Urmston, though other venues would be utilised throughout the north-west. The bid was placed in February of 1990, with the decision of the IOC being made in the September. In reality, however, Manchester was never a real contender, for it lacked both government support, and the facilities required to do justice to this prestigious sporting event. Nevertheless, the reception to Manchester's bid had been positive, and it was evident that with the appropriate backing and support, a future bid might well prove more successful. With this in mind, the City Council joined forces with the original Bid Committee and announced that together they would bid for the next games, to be held in 2000. Enthusiasm was boosted in the project when Manchester won the backing of the preferred UK location in the spring of 1991, defeating the favourite London in the process. This time, in stark contrast to the other bid, the government and the then Prime Minister, John Major, was on board. A working budget of £70 million was awarded to Manchester.

*An impressive glass wedge appeared in the heart of the city centre in the summer of 2002. As part of the regeneration of Manchester, a new urban museum – the Urbis – designated to portray life within a city, has been created. Opening initially to the media on the 11 April – where it was discovered that this has cost the Manchester taxpayers no less that £1 million! – it opened to the public on the 27 June.* The Author

East Manchester, a sector of the city that had seen much neglect through the years, was earmarked for much of the building of the proposed sports arenas, that would be required if the bid was to at least look credible. In 1992, the publication of the East Manchester Regeneration Strategy, announced an ambitious programme for redevelopment, that was sports led, though would also involve housing and business premises too. The aims were to regenerate post-industrial land, and in the process create around 10,000 new jobs. The National Cycling Centre, built in Eastlands, was just one of the positive things that came from the ambitious Olympic Bid; others would include the opening of the Intermediate Ring Road, and the commencement of construction of a National Stadium. Unfortunately, despite the best planning, ultimately, of course, Manchester failed to gain the right to stage the 2000 Olympic Games, in the end losing out to Sidney.

The knock-on effects of the bid did have a positive effect on the redevelopment of the city. The Nynex Arena (later the MEN Arena) had originally been scheduled for construction in 1989, during plans to modernise the Victoria Station, but had been cancelled due to lack of finances. The race for the 1992 Olympic Bid brought in massive funds, totalling almost £55 million, and this enabled the plans for the arena to proceed: the total cost reached £70 million, half funded by local and central government, the other half using some of the Olympic Bid funds. Work was completed in 1995, with the complex opening to the public on 15 July of that year, and has a capacity crowd of almost 20,000.

Further canalside regeneration has continued. The Bridgewater Hall, standing alongside the Rochdale Canal, was designed as a premiere concert hall, with capacity to hold almost 2500 people. It was completed and opened in 1996, with the cost jointly funded, between the Central Manchester Development Corporation and Manchester City Council, along with some European investment too.

The failure to secure the Olympics was a massive blow to Manchester. However, its conduct throughout had won the approval of the Commonwealth Games Council, who asked Manchester to bid for the forthcoming 2002 Games. London also submitted a bid for the games, though lost out to Manchester as the preferred candidate in February 1994. The decision to award the 2002 Games to Manchester came in the November of the following year. Once again the redevelopment required to host the games has had a positive knock-on effect for the city, and the games themselves raised Manchester's international profile considerably.

# Є︎PILOGUE

WHAT of twenty-first century Manchester? Although the century is still very much in its infancy, Manchester has already begun to change, with a period of regeneration and redevelopment, stemming from the 1996 IRA bomb, now beginning to show the fruits of its labour. Throughout Manchester new buildings, new shops and new homes are appearing. Manchester, with its bars and clubs has, in recent years, emerged as a twenty-four hour city – workers by day, party people by night. It is clear to say that twenty-first century Manchester will be a vibrant place in which to live and work.

During the summer of 2002, a huge glass wedge has appeared in the city centre – Urbis, is a new, interactive museum, for the new century. Using modern technology – utilising video screens and interactive displays – the visitor is informed about city life throughout the world. It is a fascinating concept, and one that is bound to attract the attention of many visitors.

However, after opening for a special viewing to the press on 11 April, the museum came under severe criticism, with the media hastily drawing attention to the £30 million spent to construct, and the fact that it will continue to cost ratepayers of Manchester no less than £1 million! Critics have already labelled Urbis as Manchester's version of the Millennium Dome! Nevertheless, since the museum opened to the public, on 27 June, it has witnessed massive attendances, and by all accounts the vast majority of the first visitors found the experience both fascinating and informative.

The Imperial War Museum North – the first of its kind outside of London – opened its doors on 5 July, and is testament to Manchester's success as a city of culture. Located alongside the Manchester Ship Canal at Trafford, this futuristic building, using three interlocking shards clad in shiny aluminium, was designed by architect Daniel Libeskind, and represents a vision of a world shattered by war. The museum will inform and educate the public in the consequences of war, utilising a mixture of static displays, large screens and interactive displays.

By far the greatest boost to Manchester's twenty-first century image has been the staging of the XVII Commonwealth Games in July 2002. Securing the Games meant that massive investment poured into Manchester, and the City Council used this wisely, locating the sporting venues in the most deprived areas of the city. East Manchester, possibly the most deprived area of the city, has benefited the most, from the construction of the City of Manchester Stadium.

To highlight the Games, and link it to the Queen's Golden Jubilee, an electronic baton was carried by volunteers around the world. On its long journey, covering 64,000 miles, it visited no less than twenty-five countries of the Commonwealth, and was carried by no less than 5000 people. The Jubilee Baton reached the north west of England in July, completing its mammoth journey at the City of Manchester Stadium on the evening of 25 July, where it was presented to the Queen. Inside the baton was a message of peace and goodwill to all the people of the Commonwealth, which Her Majesty then read to the crowd.

The XVII Commonwealth Games began with a fantastic opening ceremony at the City of Manchester Stadium. Once the Games got underway, they proved to be the best ever. Spectators were thrilled to witness a resurrection in the fortunes of the English team; overall taking second place in the final medal table to Australia. Throughout the ten day event, it has been recorded that one billion people watched the Games on television throughout the world.

The overall organisation of the Games was magnificent. For the VIP's a fleet of chauffeur driven cars had been laid on, which reached the stadium with ease as many roads had been closed especially. GMPTE ensured that people could reach the Games from far and wide through good public transport, which included the use of the Manchester Metrolink, and a fleet of special buses, drivers were asked to use the park and ride schemes to avoid congestion. It is recorded that seventy-five per cent of the public opted to use public transport.

The closing ceremony, on Sunday 4 August, was as spectacular as that of the opening – even in the midst of a constant downpour of rain, spirits were on such a high that they refused to be dampened. The spectators, both in the stadium and watching on television around the world, were witness to an event of colour and light, that offered not just entertainment but meaning – using symbols to show the varied faiths that exist within the countries of the Commonwealth, and sharing a hope of peace.

The Commonwealth Games will leave behind a legacy for the people of Manchester. It is estimated that it will produce around six thousand jobs. The Games' departure will not leave any white-elephants behind either – for the City of Manchester Stadium is set to become the new home of Manchester City Football Club, ready for use in the 2003/4 season.

And what of Manchester's ambitions to host the Olympic Games? When asked, more than a third of Mancunians thought that this was the logical next step. The City Council agreed, making suggestions that they might consider a future bid for the Olympics. However, such enthusiasm was dampened by the fact the Government announced that it did not consider a future bid for the Olympics by Manchester, either alone, or even as a joint bid between Manchester and London, to be a worthwhile consideration. Surely Manchester no-longer needs to prove itself on the world stage, it is worthy of hosting any international sporting event, from the Olympic Games to the World Cup.

So, what of twenty-first century Manchester? It is already with us – it is Manchester today – a city that has seemingly been reborn; a city of culture; a vibrant city that never sleeps; a city of sport; and yet a city that embraces its past.

# *A*CKNOWLEDGEMENTS

THIS book could not have been written were it not for the tireless service of the staff of the Local Studies Unit at Manchester Central Library, and my thanks go to them for that. I would also like to thank the staff from the following North-West libraries for supplying background information: Warrington Central Library, Liverpool Record Office, St Helens Local History Library, and the Lancashire Record Office.

The vast majority of the photographs and the picture postcards come from my own collection, though I must thank Bob Dobson for locating the illustrations: these excellent drawings appear throughout the book, though especially in the King Cotton chapter, created by H E Tidmarsh at the end of the nineteenth century and taken from the *Old and New Manchester* series of volumes.

I also have to thank the staff of Wharncliffe Books – in particular Rachael, Barbara, Sylvia, and series editor Brian Elliott – for their assistance and support throughout, making this project a reality.

And, finally, my sincere thanks to Mancunnians throughout the ages – without their interesting activities this story would not have been worth relating.

# ᔍELECT BIBLIOGRAPHY

Bolt, Geoffrey, *A Regional History of the Railways of Gt. Britain:Vol 10, The North West,* David & Charles (1978).

Carlson, Robert E, *The Liverpool & Manchester Railway Project, 1821-1831,* (David & Charles, 1975).

Donaghy, Thomas J, *Liverpool & Manchester Railway Operations, 1831-1845* (David & Charles, 1972).

Ferneyhough, Frank, *Liverpool & Manchester Railway, 1830-1980* (Robert Hale, 1980).

Gray, Edward, *The Manchester Ship Canal* (Sutton Publications, 1997).

Hadfield, Charles and Biddle, Gordon, *The Canals of North West England, volume 1,* David & Charles (1970).

Hall, Stanley, *Rail Centres: Manchester* (Ian Allen, 1995).

Hardy, Clive, *Manchester Since 1900* (Archive Publications, 1988).

HMSO, *Manchester, 50 Years of Change* (HMSO, 1995).

Kidd, Alan, *Manchester, Towns & City Histories Series* (Ryburn, 1993).

Krieger, Eric, *Bygone Manchester* (Phillimore, 1984).

Makepeace, Chris, *Manchester, Britain in Old Photographs* (Sutton Publications, 1996).

Makepeace, Chris, *More Memories of Manchester* (True North Books, 2000).

Marlow, Joyce, *The Peterloo Massacre* (Rapp & Whiting, 1969).

Messinger, Gary S, *Manchester in the Victorian Age* (Manchester University Press, 1985).

Nicholls, Robert, *Trafford Park:the first hundred years* (Phillimore, 1996).

Owen, David, *The Manchester Ship Canal* (Manchester University Press, 1983).

Reach, Angus Bethune, *Manchester and the Textile Districts* (Helmshore Local History Society, 1972).

Sanders, John, *Manchester* (Rupert Hart-Davies, 1967).

Tait, James, *Medieval Manchester and the Beginnings of Lancashire* (Manchester University Press, 1904).

Thompson, W H, *History of Manchester to 1852* (John Sherratt & Son, 1967).

Walmsley, Robert, *Peterloo: The Case Reopened* (Manchester University Press, 1969).

Wheeler, James, *Manchester* (Love & Barton, 1836).

# INDEX